The Practice of Residential Work

Also by Roger Clough:

Old Age Homes

*Residential Work**

Groups and Groupings: Life and Work in Day and Residential Settings (co-edited with A. Brown)

Practice, Politics and Power in Social Services Departments

Insights into Inspection: The Regulation of Social Care

The Abuse of Care in Residential Institutions

Care in Chaos: Frustration and Challenge in Community Care (co-authored with R. Hadley)

* also published by Macmillan

The Practice of Residential Work

Roger Clough

Consultant editor: Jo Campling

First published 2000 by
MACMILLAN PRESS LTD
Houndmills, Basingstoke, Hampshire RG21 6XS
and London
Companies and representatives
throughout the world

ISBN 0–333–66894–4 paperback

A catalogue record for this book is available
from the British Library.

This book is printed on paper suitable for recycling and
made from fully managed and sustained forest sources.

10 9 8 7 6 5 4 3 2 1
09 08 07 06 05 04 03 02 01 00

Editing and origination by
Aardvark Editorial, Mendham, Suffolk

Printed in Malaysia

Contents

Acknowledgements

The original idea for this book came from a proposal for a revised edition of *Residential Work*, which I had written for the BASW/ Macmillan series in 1982. The more I worked at the text, the more I realized that both the thinking about residential work and the context in which it is practised had changed too much to produce a revision of that text. So this is a second attempt in a very different format to write a general book about practice in residential homes.

I aim to set out theory for practice, arguing that residential work, like many other fields of work where people provide services for others, is not atheoretical. In doing so my prime acknowledgement is to many people with whom I have talked about residential practice, numerous conversations arising from work and everyday life, comments on books or lectures I have written, and my reading of academic books and novels have all contributed to my understanding.

Let me give two examples. Recently, a resident of a special housing scheme was showing me round her room, by current standards of residential homes one with plenty of space. She was sad that there was not space to bring in her books. A continuing question of mine took on a new shape: 'In such a move, what would any of us find hard in terms of maintaining our identity?'

The second example goes back 20 years to a visit to a day nursery in Bristol where the head commented as we watched some children playing: 'Some of them can't share toys until they have discovered how to play on their own.'

From such unacknowledged gems do we learn.

Formally, my thanks go to Jo Campling, the series editor for her encouragement and efficiency, the editing team at Macmillan, who do what editors should and look for infelicitous language and to the Residential Forum for permission to use material on which the Tables on pages 34 and 35 are based.

In particular I am grateful to Adrian Ward who read a very early version of the text many moons ago and suggested some reworking. David Clough and John Fletcher read drafts of Chapter 6 and made detailed suggestions.

'Thanks' to one's family never seems an adequate reward for the combination of support, debate and help with the text. Nevertheless, my thanks to my wife Ann.

ROGER CLOUGH

Introduction

Living in residential homes

Most of the people who read this book will have experiences of going into a residential home, as a worker, as a visitor or as a resident. There will be memories of the building, perhaps of smells, of noises or of the people who live and work there.

Visiting a home is powerful because we relate it to our own lives: would we want this for ourselves or those we love?

Had we all visited the same place we would have had a common experience, but would still have different perceptions: we would have noticed different aspects and formed judgements about what the home was like.

Imagine visiting different homes at the time of an evening meal. How would we assess whether the event was indicative of a place which we would regard as good? In part, our assessment depends on our own expectations. Do we prefer to eat with others or privately, at the same or different times, being served or serving ourselves, cooking part or all of the meal? How much importance do we give to the quality of the cooking, nutrition, cleanliness or decor? Would we expect differences between homes for children and young people, younger adults with learning disabilities, younger adults with physical disabilities and older adults?

It is immediately obvious that there are numerous ways of organizing mealtimes, many of which would be satisfactory, many of which would not. What form is a meal in a residential home to take? How does the style and structure of the meal fit with the function of the home? In other words we have to think about the arrangements for food in the home from the perspective both of function and of *process*. The consideration of function is examining what is wanted: what is it hoped will be achieved through the provision and eating of food? The process is the means by which the objectives are to be reached.

Any of us will know how important it is, in the place where we are living, to have food that we like. But a meal is not only an occasion for getting food inside us: frequently it is also a social experience. So, mealtimes which technically might be rated highly on the grounds that the food is good, the place is hygienic and there is plenty of choice, could be unpleasant if the way the staff talk to residents is harsh and dismissive, or residents are sitting with people whom they dislike. In fact, although the quality of the food matters, some people may rate a meal more in terms of enjoyment of others' company.

Meals illustrate the complexity of residential life: there are residents with particular needs and wants; there are the physical resources of buildings and plant; and there are the staff, the people who provide services and to some extent manage events. The production of a meal is not just a mechanical exercise. It is dependent on decisions about function which are linked to values. But having determined the type of meal, and indeed the type of experience, there has to be a system to produce the desired end.

Residential work is about this interplay between people and systems. If a residential home is to be purposeful, then much of the strength of the establishment will be found in the ways in which daily living events are managed. Many of these events require staff to be involved in the personal, physical care of residents, such as getting up, washing, going to the lavatory, going to bed or to meals. The way in which this care is provided will affect the well-being of the resident.

So, residential work is about practical and mundane tasks, which themselves are integral to creating an environment in which people can lead satisfactory lives.

Anyone who lives or works in places which are called 'residential homes', will know something of the *potential* of residential work: the provision of building and services in a way which allows the residents to live their lives as fully as possible. Residential workers have an opportunity both to structure services and to be alongside people. It is in this combination of practical task and personal relationship that the opportunity lies for purposeful and valuable work.

Deliberately I start with the potential: the potential for individualized and warm physical care, for residents to feel cared for, for some residents to find the space to review their lives and find new ways of managing. It is not fanciful to claim that residential work may allow, indeed create an environment for the healing of troubled minds, the development of new skills or the establishment of feelings of security, dignity and warmth that comes from the best of personalized care. One of my tasks in this book is to capture the hope, vision and opportunity of residential work *and* to examine ways of achieving these.

Good residential work is a *craft* and does not just happen. The people who work in residential homes have to develop and refine skills. In addition they must be aware of the significance of themselves, their own feelings and attitudes, when they are working alongside others. Residential work, like many other forms of work in which a central part of the task is being with other people (whether they are pupils, patients, clients, service users or residents), demands a conscious use of self.

What then is this activity which I term 'residential work'? The importance of the question lies in the consequences of the answer for the analysis of residential work and thus for the identification of the skills of workers.

I shall be arguing in this book that 'residential work', although akin to many other work groups, is best seen as a type of *direct care*, that is work which has as a central aspect the direct physical care of other people. It involves working with people to maintain their lives. The fact of residence makes this work different from home care, and the need for direct care distinguishes the work from special housing and hotels. The implications of this for the work identity and training of people who work in residential homes will be pursued.

I shall be contending also that staff need training. The argument is based on a premise, first, that an understanding of people and their circumstances has the potential to improve practice and, second, that skills can be learnt. Furthermore, it is essential that staff adhere to acceptable values about the worth of those who live in homes and the worth of their own work. Usually people are horrified to discover that most staff working in residential homes have no training: they had presumed both that staff were trained and that training provides some guarantee of quality.

Theory can – and should – inform practice. A core task in this book is to examine the theories which are useful for residential work. Of course, residential homes differ one from another in objectives and style and it is unproductive to write of residential work as if it is the same in all places. There are aspects of residential work which are common in all places, such as the recognition that the arrangements for daily living are intrinsic to the meeting of grand objectives. However, the notion of 'generic residential work' attempts to force too much conformity on places which are very different from one another. My approach is to highlight common themes, such as the significance of the journeys people travelled in becoming residents, while recognizing that the experiences of individuals and groups will differ widely.

My aim is to show the relevance of theory to practice. I see the book as potentially useful to practitioners, to managers and perhaps to residents. The core readers are likely to be students training to work in residential homes, although I think it useful also for those whose work impinges on residential work and who would benefit from a fuller understanding of task and practice: social workers, teachers or nurses for example. Different people may wish to find different routes through the book. For example, Chapter 7, Researching Residential Life, will be more directly useful for those who want to think about undertaking research in a residential home or to examine the validity of research findings which they read. But managers or residents might want to consider how they should respond to requests for research in their home. The last two chapters, Managing in a Residential Home and Good Enough Lifestyles, may be less relevant to care workers than to managers. Chapter 6, An Ethical Base for Practice, looks at values and at philosophy.

I have a strongly held view that theories are of no use to practitioners unless they inform and, consequently improve, practice. To accomplish that they must make sense to the people who are to use them. Theories should not be written as if they were intellectual barricades, designed by their language and formula to exclude most people. The best theories are those which help us to a new understanding of our world. Thus in one home for older adults which I studied, staff were insistent that residents could call on staff at any time during the night. Yet few did so. I observed incidents in which staff talked to residents about their work the previous night. They commented on the nuisance of some residents who had kept pressing the call bell. Residents who heard this would learn that the formal statement 'Call us at any time' had to be interpreted in the light of the informal labelling of some residents as a nuisance.

One test for this book is whether ideas which may be complex are written about in a way which helps them to be understood. The same test applies to students and workers: that theories are written about and discussed in ways which share knowledge rather than develop mystique. I draw on evidence from research and theorizing and from people's accounts of residential life. I use my own ideas and experiences as well as those of others. What is important for the reader of any text is to examine the nature of the evidence on which conclusions are drawn. Thus, an insight from experience (our own or those of others) may help in examining and understanding. But it must not be relied on as 'truth', for it has to be tested as to its generalizability.

The language which we use to describe the activity of residential work is indicative of how we see the task. In the title I have used the term 'residential *work*', to describe the task which goes on in residential homes. In other parts of the book I have written about 'residential *care*'. It is often difficult to capture, in a phrase, different elements of an activity. Within the vast range of types of residential homes, are substantial variations in function: as a consequence, the relationships between residents and other residents or staff will also vary substantially.

The term 'care' suggests either that one person has an interest in the welfare of another or that the person is doing something for another, in the sense of looking after that person. One recent study contends that older people in their own homes prefer to think of those who provide domiciliary services as helpers rather than carers (Clark *et al.*, 1998). The point being made is that 'being "looked after" can symbolize loss of independence. Providers should be sensitive in their use of language' (Rowntree, 1999). Given that I argue later in the book that many older people see the move to a residential home as a symbol of giving up, the notion of 'being looked after' may not be helpful.

Yet, residential work at its best provides care in both senses and, for the time being I continue to use the phrase 'residential care'. In thinking about the task, and in working with people in residential homes, it is imperative to remind ourselves that the activity is centred on *assisting* people with various aspects of their lives. Thus, the task is concerned with supporting people to develop, maintain or recover their management of their lives. Of course, on some occasions, some people's capacity to direct their lives may be very limited.

Before starting to consider the journeys of residents, a few words on my own 'work journey'. My first jobs were in approved schools, as a housemaster and teacher with adolescent boys from 16 to 19. Most of the rest of my work life has been spent in lecturing to and writing for residential workers and social workers. I distinguish the two because when I started lecturing residential workers, whether with children and young people or adults, were not termed social workers. For four years from 1990 I worked in a newly formed registration and inspection unit. Currently, once again I am working at a university as a lecturer and researcher.

My own history has an impact on my perception. In particular, two points should be noted. First, my own direct experience was as a worker in residential child care a long time ago. Second, most of my research, writing and teaching has been related to residential work with children or older people. I have read about, visited and worked with

students and staff from other residential homes but have less know
ledge and experience of their practice. This book is designed as a
general text but, inevitably, draws on my expertise. Throughout the text
I have tried to show the source of information and the way in which it
can be considered for its relevance in other settings.

I have no doubt that residential homes can be life enhancing. I have
no doubt of the importance to residents of the ways in which staff work
with residents. And I have no doubt that the best practice does not just
happen as a result of innate skills: it is built on a search to understand.

1

Living in a Residential Home

Journeys to residence

In order to examine practice in a residential home we have to know about the journeys which people have made to arrive there. Residents come with their history of people, places and events to an establishment which also has its history. What happens in a residential home can only be understood properly with this link between person and home.

The notion of a journey also captures other dimensions. The fact that someone lives in a residential home was not an inevitability: a process has taken place with events, reflections and decisions.

> Mr Jepson had some knowledge of the home to which he had moved from visiting friends. He described the day at his own home when he had been 'reading the Sunday paper and the floor came up to him'. His son had said that something must be done and he had seen a doctor at the hospital.
>
> Mr Jepson's son, a man in his 50s, wrote of the reasons why Mr Jepson had moved into a home. 'My wife died some three years previously of cancer and it became impossible for me to keep house for an aged father and myself when his medical condition became so unpredictable.' He had sometimes felt sad about his father's move. 'Probably a little self-pity. A very happy family shattered by a mother dying of thrombosis, wife of cancer and father becoming degenerate.' (adapted from Clough, 1981, p. 118)

The process by which an individual comes to be seen, by self or others, as someone who might move to a residential home is a significant one. First, a view develops that the person is unable to cope or unlikely to survive in the current environment, because of incapacity and/or the effects of behaviour on self or others. At some stage these views of 'inability to cope or survive' will be examined and there will be consideration of what should happen.

The move from identification of a problem to arrival at a residential home is often presented as a rational process in which a profile of the individual is assembled and a place is found that matches what the person wants and needs. What is referred to as 'assessment' may be a full profile of an individual including capacity and skills as well as problems or it may be little more than a brief account of someone's problems with minimal comment from the individual. Such accounts may be used to justify decisions rather than to examine options. The best assessment is formed from a struggle to understand and interpret, a struggle in which the individual and significant others as well as workers participate. The way in which the assessment is carried out will influence the route that the person will take. The reasons for moving to a home and the process will vary with different resident groupings.

There is evidence that the idea of matching what someone needs with a particular place may be hard to achieve. For example, social services staff, wanting to find the appropriate specialist residential establishment for children and young people, may have very limited knowledge of places. Attempting to find out about places may be haphazard (Clough, 1996c). Of course having found what is judged the best place, there may be no vacancy.

Frequently, decisions are hurried as there is a tendency for people to move into a residential home when in a crisis.

The extent to which an individual is involved in the process which leads to a move into a residential home has immense impact on their stay in the establishment. For example, typically, the moves of older people into residential homes will have been initiated by others: relatives, doctors, community nurses or social workers. In addition only a minority of older people play any significant part in the choice of the particular home to which they move. It is useful to consider the process for younger adults and young people. How far have adults who moved from large hospitals to smaller homes had a say in whether they wanted such a move, where they were to live or, importantly, with whom they were to live?

A move to a residential home is likely to be the consequence of some problems in people's lives. Whatever the potential in the changed circumstances for improvement, change in itself brings questions as to one's past and future lifestyle, perhaps about identity and worth. The relationship of individuals to the buildings in which they live has altered:

> It is this changed relationship which holds the key to other dynamics: to residents' construction and management of identity; their relationships with other residents

and staff; and their negotiation about lifestyle and services. The key factor is that residents do not feel the same about themselves nor do they feel the same relationship to the world in a residential home as they do in their own house. The feeling is that you have moved into someone else's territory. (Clough, 1998a, pp. 1–3)

Daily life: theory related to daily events

Mr Jepson talked about a typical day. He liked getting up, though getting out of bed was a problem. 'Everything brings back memories.' 'Getting to the lavatory is difficult... I get a paper, don't read it much. I smoke a pipe sometimes but often don't feel like it. We watch TV from about four to nine or ten thirty. I don't talk much, watch what's going on up the street. Very often think "What did you come here for?" I try to answer the conundrum... I come up to the room with everybody asleep, there's no fun in it, though I might sleep from eleven to twelve. The atmosphere is very subdued. Nobody stands up to sing a song of sixpence... What worries me most is not walking.'

He said that he would advise a friend to move in to the home because he found everything 'puck-a-doo'. 'What's the good of being in the outside world when there's somewhere to rest your weary head?'

Mrs Williams listened to the radio in the morning from 7.30. At home she used to stay in bed a bit longer, about nine. She found it quite easy to get dressed but did not like to get down too early to meals and have to wait like school children. She enjoyed meals and helped afterwards with drying up. She enjoyed knitting and would sit outside in the summer. She was glad to have her health and strength and be happy. She knitted in the sitting room and took an interest in other people. On some days she would visit the local town, though grumbled that she had to stay out too long as she knew so many people and had to stop and talk. (adapted from Clough, 1981, pp. 118–30)

Mr Jepson and Mrs Williams *lived* in a home for older people. In so doing, they undertook many of the same tasks as they would have done in their own homes. Some were concerned with the mechanics of existence: getting up and going to bed, eating, washing, going to the toilet. Others were related to the sorts of contacts they wanted to make with other people or the activities which they wanted to pursue.

Of course, all of these events will vary with what individuals want, with their state of health and with their resources. However, life in the home will vary also with what those who manage the home see as the function and style of the home. There is no one correct way to run a home whether for adults or children. Yet what is vital in all homes is an understanding of the link between function, objectives and the arrangements for daily living.

Good residential life is built on creating a lifestyle in which residents can live to the full. It is dependent on thought-out practice in daily events: (i) *routines*; (ii) *managing daily life*; (iii) *caring for self and possessions*; and (iv) *activities*.

Routines: the daily round

Events are repeated at differing intervals. The provisions of meals or drinks happen several times a day, often at regular times. Bathing takes place less often. By contrast, activities such as going to the lavatory, occur throughout the day but not at set times and not for all residents at the same time. Routines are in fact a part of 'the daily round', a phrase in a hymn by George Herbert which captures a day's cyclical nature.

I am using the word 'routine' to convey something that happens on a regular basis. In this sense it is a neutral word, neither indicating that the activity is good nor bad. Some writing on residential care has assumed that doing things at fixed times indicates regimentation. This may be the case, but is not necessarily so. Most people want a pattern to their day with events that are familiar or take place at set times. These can help provide security or a shape to the day. They may become valued rituals. Reflection on the patterns of our own days will illustrate how we construct our day, perhaps to mark a change from one activity to another or as something to look forward to. Indeed, routines have potential value for reviewing the past and for living in the present. Most of us want a balance between consistency and flexibility.

The test of whether the style of daily life is appropriate or not is whether it is institution driven or resident driven. One of the dangers in residential homes is that regimentation takes over: the imperative to get the work done gets in the way of personalized care. In households, a measure of organization is needed to ensure that the housework is done, and done at times that match the arrangements for living. There has to be far more planning in a residential home if the cleaning or the cooking are to be done in the way that is wanted: without planning, the job gets out of control. But planning does not have to drive out spontaneity.

Mrs Williams was in the sitting room one day and told me that she had to go and have a bath. She did not want to because she had a bad cold but said 'I've got to go and have a bath – I don't want to, still I suppose I've got to obey orders.' She went to the bathroom door, knocked and told the assistant 'Matron says it's all right for me to have a bath' (Clough, 1981, p. 124). It would seem from this conversation that Mrs Williams thought the decision as to whether or not to bath was that of the staff, not hers. It sounds as if there was too little flexibility.

To plan well for events like these it is necessary to be aware of the feelings that such activities typically generate. Mr Jepson said, 'Everything brings back memories.' Doing familiar things in another place, in a different way and with new people inevitably reminds us of changes in our life. Importantly, such changes can become valuable in their own right.

Meals are an example of a routine activity. There is no single, correct way of making arrangements for such events, although some key factors can be listed:

- *the function of meals needs to be defined and fit with the function of the home*: what are seen as the key values and objectives in the home? how are mealtimes to help the realization of those objectives?

- *systems have to be developed to produce desired ends*: arrangements have to be made to determine the format of meals and then to decide menus, purchase food, cook, serve and wash up;

- *there should be negotiation about both function and system between residents, staff and other interested parties*: what part may residents play in decisions in the home, whether about timing, food, or where to have the meal? people have different views on what they want from a meal in terms of food and socializing; there are also considerations of what is the responsibility of staff in the sense of a duty of care, which will vary with different types of home; all homes should provide a good diet but the extent to which residents should be free to eat what they want, should be negotiated in each home;

- *account should be taken of majority and individual interests*: an easy statement but one that demands an understanding of the importance of culture; thus, what may be wanted is not only a vegetarian dish but one that is prepared in a particular way;

- *meals evoke strong memories*: of particular people and episodes, and of the comfort, pleasures and dislikes associated with food; eating as an adult when you are not able to manage to eat on your own, will evoke memories of childhood;

- *there are constraints to the production of meals in terms of equipment, buildings and budget.*

We should recognize also that some of what is wanted in terms of objectives is a by product and cannot be achieved directly. Pick (1981) writes of mealtimes: 'These were fields of expression, discovery, sharing, discussion, disagreement, tolerance, vehemence.' The task is to create the preconditions for people to feel secure in risking opinions, to enjoy a meal and to have sufficient enjoyment. In planning there may be a vision of some of what will happen; one of the joys of residential life is that people and events have lives of their own.

The kernel of good residential work is that the life of the place is planned so that the interests of individuals will be met. This will and must be done differently in each place because residents, staff and management will try to achieve their aims in different ways. Thus in one home it may be decided that residents will meet together for an evening meal: the place has been established around a particular idea of community and the regular sharing of a meal. Another place will be structured so that residents may choose between meals in their own rooms or in a restaurant, cooking or not, and whether to eat alone or with other residents. Alternatively, at a residential school where it is thought that the children have difficulties in setting appropriate boundaries to their behaviour, staff might serve the children to ensure that there is control.

But the common feature of a residential home and the one which distinguishes it say from a hotel is that the arrangements for living are structured to take account of the special wants and needs of residents.

Managing daily life

For many residents, daily living events demand more attention than formerly: they are daily episodes which have to be managed rather than undertaken en route to doing something else.

The events are ones that require practical skills and efficiency: meals cooked well and ready on time or residents helped in and out of the bath with skilled help so that they feel safe. However, the events have psychological significance both in relation to the present and the past.

Take the process of waking in the morning and getting up. A teenager, feeling defeated and worthless, may see little point in getting up. Bed is warm and comforting. Adolescence is in any case likely to be a time of mixed emotions in the move from young person to adult. Young people in residential homes are particularly likely to face uncertainties as to whether they want to grow up and confront what seems a hostile world.

Many people in residential homes will feel less constrained than those outside homes by the external commitments of school and work. For certain people this makes the management of each day difficult. Freed from the necessity of getting up for specific events, people have to face more of a daily decision as to whether they want to get up.

Some adults will have been awake for long spells in the night, perhaps with discomfort or anxiety: they may be glad to get up or may feel depressed and not wish to move. For each of us, getting up means a move to tackling the events of the day. Residents may feel less confident than they were of their identity or sense of worth: they may not want to move into a new day.

Others, young people or adults, may be fearful of letting go at night. Again, the reasons will be diverse but staff need to recognize that people may be uneasy or frightened. Going to sleep is a nightly act of trust that it is all right to let go.

Other daily living events will touch individuals in different ways. Bathing and washing may seem a chore, a comfort or an anxiety. But such intimate physical care also means individuals have to be helped with activities which have been managed privately since they were children, unless shared with close friends. Remembrances are all powerful: of dependency, embarrassment, feelings as a man or woman as to care by someone of the same or different sex. Staff, faced with the regularity of such work, may forget these deep-rooted feelings.

The move to a residential home has an impact on people's management of their lives. One way for staff to help residents consider how they want to live is to talk to residents about their lives before they came into the home:

- What did they do at different times?
- What did they find difficult and how did they cope?
- What were the high spots of the day?
- How did they manage particular events, whether to do with looking after oneself (washing or putting on shoes) or going to bed and sleeping?

It makes a huge difference to people's lives in the residential home if they are able to work out over time how they want to live. The danger is that patterns are set early on, and that residents change their way of life not because of what they want but because of what they think is expected of them; they feel that they must stop doing something in the way they did because they are embarrassed about staff or residents seeing their struggle to manage. Some of the investment in looking after oneself and some of the good parts of a day may get lost. New residents need to be able to work out how they want to live, which may involve stopping doing some things which were painful or worrying, maintaining some of their former coping mechanisms and finding new ones.

If staff recognize the threat to identity that a move to a residential home introduces, they will be better placed to review both practices within the home and their own interaction with residents. New residents experience a major life change. Staff will need to be sensitive to the experience of becoming a resident so that residents can reflect and re-establish their perception of self. The importance is that much of that perception is founded in daily living activities: in getting up, eating, washing, choosing one's clothes, keeping house, receiving visitors, talking directly or on the phone, doing things on one's own or with others. The way in which these events are managed, including the way in which people talk to each other while they are happening, influences perception of self.

Caring for self and possessions

The way we dress, do our hair, indeed smell are all indicators to others of how we perceive ourselves or what we want to show to others. Within the residents' private space, that is particularly in bedrooms, the same will be true of the presentation of the room: what do people want to have around? Indeed, a person's sense of identity will influence whether they want to make their mark on the place where they live.

Looking after clothes is of more significance than often recognized: washing and mending clothes; buying new clothes; and choosing what to wear for particular occasions. One of the aspects that distresses relatives most when visiting family members in residential homes is if they find the person in clothes that are not theirs and are judged inappropriate: 'She would never have worn that', they may say. The identity of the person has been called into question. Even if not stated, the same is likely to be happening to the resident if the clothes seem wrong. Some residents may be depressed and stop bothering what they look like. They do not mind that clothes have food spilled on them, that their hair is unkempt or that not washing frequently is leading to their smell being commented on by others. Another group will be struggling with their identity: perhaps young people or adults with learning disabilities who are living in a home for the first time.

Even the manner in which clothes are selected to be worn has an effect on the resident. Should adults with learning disabilities be allowed to wear clothes that would be judged inappropriate for adults and might lead to others laughing at them? The set of ideas which has been termed *normalization* has as a premise that people's status in the eyes of others will be affected by what they do, including the way they present themselves. On the one hand notions of *self-determination* and *choice* would lead to the individual making the decision; on the other, it could be argued that the person does not fully understand the consequence of wearing childish clothes and that it is in her/his interests to avoid further negative stereotyping.

In each example there is no one right way of working. The task for staff is to recognize that what might seem insignificant has a far wider impact on people's lives.

Activities

Under the heading *activities* I include structured groups where people meet for a set purpose (such as pottery, current affairs or keep fit classes) and unstructured happenings that take place between other set events: what people do between getting up and breakfast, or breakfast and lunch, talking to other people over coffee, reading, gardening or watching TV. Anyone who has visited residential homes is likely to have seen activities that seem satisfactory, even life enhancing, and others that appear demeaning, stultifying or deadening. What factors tend to lead to any of these outcomes?

One consideration is the lifestyle of similar people in their own home. What do people do when on their own? This tests what is happening against people's interest, ability and life-stage. There are dangers in forgetting that much of any of our lives may appear drab and uninviting to others, and even ourselves. How much time do we spend watching TV programmes that are filling in time because we cannot decide what else to do? Adolescents in their own homes may spend a lot of time sitting around playing computer games or listening to music. But that knowledge of normal adolescence and of how others live should not excuse staff from thinking about how to create in a residential home a place where people can live as fully as possible.

In addition to considering *what* people do, it is worth examining *the process by which they decide* what to do. This is not easy to unravel because of the pressure to conform that so many of us feel in a new environment. Probably, it is advantageous for a new resident not to adopt a permanent pattern to the day too soon and to experiment with different activities.

Another influence on activity is the environment. One of the opportunities of residential life is for residents to meet others and to do things which cannot be done in one's own home. So the lifestyle should not aim to repeat what may have been a drab or unhappy lifestyle from the person's own home. The environment is important. Cairns and Cairns (1989) drawing on Maier (1981, p. 40) state:

> The size and shape of room, lighting, heating, furnishing, outlook, the pictures and objects within the room, will all influence the ease or otherwise with which the group feels comfortable with itself. (p. 176)

They go on to describe the planning of their home: the kitchen as a focal point, open fires, thick carpeting, heavy curtains, wood furniture and large cushions. 'Even teenagers often seem immediately more relaxed with a large cushion on their laps' (p. 178).

> Finally: there are pictures on the walls, glassware and pottery on the shelves, musical instruments, records and tapes, and, above all, books in their hundreds, and a constant stream of newspapers and magazines, all for the using. Sooner or later every child's curiosity is aroused by something; chance remarks, throwaway questions start us all searching through shelves on an impromptu voyage of discovery that leads, as often as not, to self-discovery. (p. 178)

Contrast that picture with the living rooms in so many residential homes. The design and organization of the home have a direct impact on what people do when they are not involved in more structured episodes of living such as meals.

Some activities are semi-structured, taking place at set times or for set groups. Classes in crafts, music or physical fitness all come under this heading. I have seen events where the quality of the work is impressive and the attitude to the members is as learner participants. I have seen other groups where what happens makes me cringe: adults appear to be treated like pre-school children, praised for making shapes out of toilet-roll holders or such like. In the latter, staff seem to be patronizing to the adult participants. Some activity which goes under a title of 'reminiscence work' is similarly belittling.

The first cautionary note from this is be aware that the existence of an activity class is not necessarily a good thing: what matters is the quality of the activity. Some of the factors that appear to distinguish good from poor activity groups are that:

- the teachers are skilled: they know about their subject;
- the language used in the title of the activity and in the event itself emphasizes learning;
- stereotypes about learning are avoided: young people who have failed in their early education may thrive when they are ready to learn; younger and older adults can and do learn new skills, although their techniques for learning may change from those they used earlier;
- the materials should differ from the sort of recycled products used in playgroups, so that the activities differ from those undertaken by children;
- people should have their interest stimulated rather than be manipulated to join in.

Another example would concern a keep fit group. It is clear that it is valuable to get people to exercise muscles. Many of us get such exercise (insofar as we do!) from daily events such as housework, looking after ourselves, gardening, even moving from one place to another. One approach to keeping fit would be to see whether there is potential to stimulate more natural activity of this type within the home. If keep fit classes are to be held, then the activities need to be thought out carefully. The staff approach has to be skilful if the sort of patronizing and demeaning episodes described above are to be avoided. There are many different approaches: people exercising on their own, as happens in a gym or swimming pool, or in small groups; or staff working with individuals in relaxation, massage and exercise. Activities must enhance rather than diminish people's dignity and sense of self-worth. Some people do not want to go to classes where their performance or physique can be judged or tested against that of others.

Residential living – not what we dream of for ourselves or for those whom we love

By and large people do not want to live in residential homes themselves and do not see it as the best way of life for people about whom they care.

It is important to remind ourselves of this reality because there is a temptation in trying to counter the prevalent negative image of residential life, to assert too much in terms of either its potential or attractiveness. I write as someone who is strongly committed to a view that residential homes can be good places in which to live and that, for some people, at some stages in their lives, they are the best choice. That must not mask the fact that as we think ahead about our lives, we hope that we will not move into a residential home. The same is true for those whom we love: by and large we hope that our children as young people or adults, our siblings, our partners or our parents will not move into a residential home.

Typically, the explanations given for the unattractiveness of residential homes are linked to the inadequacies of the current lifestyle of those who live in them or the perceptions arising from the legacy of former harsher regimes. Both have substance. In part the current image of residential homes is a consequence of the past. In the nineteenth century there was a principle which has become known as that of *less eligibility* which aimed at ensuring that life within the workhouse was not more attractive than that available to the lowest paid person in work outside the workhouse. Life in the workhouse was to be 'less eligible' than that outside to ensure that too many people were not attracted into the residential home.

In the last 50 years much analysis of residential homes has focused on their dysfunctional aspects. It is argued that they have stripped residents (and perhaps staff) of identity, have regimented and have controlled people's lives. Indeed, it has been claimed that residential establishments provided services in ways which have come to be termed 'institutionalized': that is, the routines and good functioning of the establishment took priority over the interests of individuals. More recently there have been revelations of serious malpractice and abuse in some homes.

Nevertheless, there is a fundamental aspect of attitudes to residential homes that has nothing to do with what happens within them. People move into residential homes when a cluster of circumstances has led them or others to conclude that they cannot cope in the place where, currently, they are living. In ignorance of our own future life circumstance, it is hard to plan for a time when a cluster of circumstances makes our current living arrangements no longer viable and aspects that are central to our lives are gone: our capacity to look after ourselves or those we love, to decide what we want to do and to be with the people whom we love. Thus a part of the negative image of residential homes is a negative image of an unwelcome life-stage, almost one which we cannot contemplate.

Residential life for anyone in a welfare establishment signifies that an alternative has had to be found to what are presumed to be the normal and the best arrangements for living, that is living in one's own house with responsibility for self and others. Independence is prized, coupled with self-sufficiency. Payne (1995, p. 108) contends that the main priority of the community care service is to maintain the client's independence. Residential life indicates that this has gone wrong, that this type of 'normal' living cannot be maintained. Thus it is a visible indicator to self and others of one's current capacity and status.

The title of the Wagner committee report of 1988, *A Positive Choice*, makes a bold claim that people should move into residential homes as a positive choice. It was intended as a counter to the prevalent negative view of residential living. There is also much writing which recognizes that, typically, most people do not want to move into a residential home. The research evidence today recognizes the continuing reality that, except in a few situations, older people do not want to move into residential homes (Sinclair, 1988b, 1998c, pp. 46, 247). Indeed, Sinclair claimed that 'they are not places in which residents can live normal or reasonable lives' (1988b, p. 46). This is recognized, even if somewhat superficially, in the NHS and Community Care Act 1990 with its related guidance. Griffiths (1988) in a report preceding the Act stated that people should be 'helped to stay in their own homes for as long as possible', with residential and nursing home care reserved for those whose needs cannot be met in any other way.

The Children Act 1989 with its related guidance places emphasis on people staying within their families whenever possible. In some ways the statements about young people and adults appear to be both straightforward and sensible; indeed they challenge properly any tendency for people to be moved into a residential home when they do not want it, in particular if the only reason for the move to a residential home is that it seems easier than finding other ways of resolving a problem.

When a child or young person is unable to continue living at home (in the judgement either of the family or the social services department) fostering has been the preferred form of care. The failings of fostering have tended to be ignored (see Berridge, 1997).

The important point in relation to residential care is that it is rarely seen as a good specialist resource, as would a good residential school, hospital or hospice. The key question should be: if we, or those for whom we care, are unable to manage aspects of our lives independently, what is the best combination of housing and services?

The question can be asked directly of oneself. What sort of service and care would I want in the following circumstances for myself, as an adult, if:

- I couldn't cook, bath, or dress myself?
- I was a risk to self or others?
- My partner died, I was a long way from my children or did not want to live with them or they with me?
- I had dementia?
- I was judged by others to be occasionally or permanently incompetent?

Or we could consider the services we would want for our children if:

- they were beyond our control;
- they were deeply hurt or traumatized and we were unable to help them;
- their delinquency was a danger to themselves or others.

The failure to recognize the significance of life events has led to a distorted analysis of attitudes to residential homes. A comparison with physical illness may be useful. We hope not to be faced with serious or chronic illness. In the main we do not plan for, and certainly do not want to go into, hospital. The reasons lie both in the largely unpredictable nature of illness and in its unpleasant, painful, frightening and life-threatening aspects. The events that lead to a move to a residential home are of the same order:

- they cannot be predicted for individuals, even though it is possible to predict the numbers of people, for example, who will suffer from dementia;
- they are likely to be consequent on the breakdown of existing patterns of living, and may well be intertwined with the circumstances of other close family members;
- they are frightening, for they threaten perception of self as a functioning member of society;
- people have no way of knowing how they or others will cope with accumulated losses or difficulties.

The current approach to residential homes regards them as a facility to be avoided both in terms of cost and because they tend to be seen as the least attractive option. Since an objective of welfare policies is to keep people out of residential homes, then those who move into a residential home do so in greater states of need and dependency than formerly. In these circumstances it is not surprising that moves to residential homes are fraught with problems.

Moves to residential homes in old age typify many of these factors. Moving house is stressful at any time of life. There are some factors which counteract such stress (Clough, 1993). For example, moves made in advance of an immediate crisis allow people greater opportunity to make decisions when they have maximum control first of investigating and consideration of options and, second, of the planning of decisions. People are happier with decisions, even when difficult, when they have played a full part in their making. Further, a move when comparatively independent allows for one's own development of lifestyle in the new area: patterns to the day, places to visit and, in particular, contacts with people. The very measures which would make residential homes more acceptable (such as the exercise of more control by prospective residents or the use of residential homes by a larger section of the population), are ruled out by a policy direction which aims to avoid the use of residential homes if at all possible. Two potentially conflicting processes exist alongside each other, the one to promote residential care as a positive resource to be used only as the option of choice, the other to keep people out of residential homes for as long as possible.

Residential homes, in contrast to some other lifestyles, tend to diminish status. They suggest something of the reality of the life circumstances of those who live there, perhaps dependence on others in some aspects of one's life, inability to cope or troublesome behaviour. Some people feel strongly that to live in a residential home implies that one's family does not care sufficiently, that one must be unlovable or that needing help implies failure.

> There is a strategy, which I shall call distancing, which asserts the difference of people who need help from ourselves. Mrs Williams, …told me that she found it difficult to be in the home because some years ago she used to come in at Christmas to sing to the residents at the very home where she now lived. She had changed role from a 'singer' to a 'sung at'. (Clough, 1996a, p. 3)

Staff work, and residents live, in a place which is seen as an unattractive option. That is not to say that some people do not want to live in residential homes; it is simply to recognize the unpalatable.

Yet some types of residential life do not carry the same stigma as residential homes: student hostels or boarding schools would be two examples. Two interconnected factors appear to be at play. First, those places which are used in more normal circumstances or are used by a prestigious or selected group appear to confer status. Second, the very fact of being in part dependent on others or unable to cope results in stereotyping and lowers the status of those who live there. The status is attached not to the residential life but to the reason for being in residence. For adults at least, the extent to which one remains in control of aspects of one's life appears significant in the conferring of status. The corollary of this is that assumptions may be made about lifestyle as a consequence of such attribution of status, regardless of whether the quality of care is good or bad. Much of what is disparaged in welfare type residential establishments for children and young people is tolerated when the establishments are chosen for other reasons. For example, residential life in boarding schools may well be more institutionalized than that in children's homes.

Residential living

People live in a residential home; for the time being it is their home. Some young people or adults will move to a residential home as a permanent place of residence, in the sense that the home becomes their permanent base or 'home'. Others will live in a residential home for a short period, knowing that it is a temporary base.

Whether their stay is permanent or temporary, residents have to do certain things. Some are concerned with the mechanics of existence: getting up and going to bed, eating, washing, going to the toilet. Others are related to the sorts of contacts residents want to make with other people or the sorts of activities which they want to pursue. Of course all of these events will vary with what individuals want for themselves, their state of health and their resources.

For numerous reasons, assisting others is not always straightforward. People may be resentful when they need help, perhaps with a measure of ambivalence towards receiving help, particularly in a society where independence is cherished.

To proceed further into understanding the nature of the work it is necessary to pick up again on the characteristics of the residents. In one way or another they are people who have found some difficulty in managing aspects of their lives; they may well be dependent on others for basic physical assistance. This makes residents different from hotel guests or schoolchildren who are not at the hotel or school because of an inability to manage part of their lives. Young people in residential homes have been described as 'troubled or troublesome' and as 'villains, victims or volunteers'. Adults are sometimes termed vulnerable, challenging or dependent.

The characteristics of 'being a resident' will be followed up in different places in this book. At this stage it is worth noting that people live in residential homes because they need (or are thought to need) some resource from the home; one consequence of such reliance on others for services is that the people who provide the services have considerable power.

If the residents are compared to people who use many other institutions from schools to hospitals, they are likely to be less able to chart their own way through the facility. In schools there will be good and bad teachers, good and bad buildings, good and bad plant. In part pupils in ordinary schools survive and thrive (if they do) because schooling is thought of as life enhancing and because they have the strengths (from themselves or their families) to find a good enough route through the snakes and ladders of education. The task is of a different order for those who live in residential homes.

One of the dilemmas in residential work has been to define what is special and distinctive about its craft: how does it differ from what parents do in families, or what is carried out in a variety of establishments from boarding schools to hotels? There is a danger of claiming too much or too little. There is a danger also of generalizing, of fitting residents or homes into neat boxes.

Unless residents are required to live in a residential home as a consequence of a legal order there should be some level of agreement between resident and staff as to function and style. This fundamental agreement does not mean that residents must agree every staff action. Rather residents must be in sympathy with the aims and the practices of the establishment. Precisely what that agreement is will need to be determined in each place.

More closely related to the individual resident, there needs to be a general agreement as to the care and treatment of that person. Sometimes ideas like this are referred to as a contract. A contract may

capture what I am describing provided it includes debate and negotiation and provided that it does not lead to a legalistic approach to direct
care. In so far as possible and appropriate, the individual should be
supported in the way she or he wishes.

Some residents will be less certain of what they want. They may feel
confused, upset or troubled. Another potential of residential life
becomes apparent. The provision of good physical care may contribute
to individuals valuing themselves and to creating an environment in
which people review their own behaviour or their relationships with
others. For example, at a mealtime the combination of reliability of
provision with a good experience may lead, whether or not staff are
present, to significant discussions between people. The environment in
which this may happen is created by a combination of individual-
centred care and stability.

Thus in all residential homes there is a mix of physical care, holding
and development of self. Analysis and categorization risk losing the
richness of residential work which lies in the combination of mundane
and significant. Residential workers, in some ways like parents or
carers in households, can respond to people in everyday activities in
ways which are therapeutic or life enhancing. Residential care should
provide a good place to live.

2

The Staff and the Organizations in which they Work

The impact of the work on staff

Working in a residential home is not the same as working in domicil-iary settings, that is in family households, although there may be some of the same characteristics. Staff witness and at times are part of other people's lives. They will see residents as they live their lives: getting up, bathing and eating; relaxing and busy; happy and sad; angry, confused or excited.

In a study of a home for older people (Clough, 1981), I have written of the way in which staff were affected by their feelings for and about residents. One person wrote of her 'distress' when a resident went to hospital because she thought that there was very little chance of him coming back (p. 139). She described another occasion:

> I sat on the floor enjoying the sun and had a chat with the men. Mr Peat is still very withdrawn but I feel he is happy in his own way. I asked him to go to the dentist but he really does not want to, he is happy chewing away with one tooth. Always get a laugh with Mr Murphy. Mr Fothergill has lost some of his spirit, I don't think he's so well.

> Joe, my heart aches for him... I must make a point of telling the night staff he needs help in the morning... I really admire his courage. (p. 205)

The job is emotionally as well as physically demanding. As one care assistant said: 'Sometimes you're so tired after a day here, trying to get people to walk and so on'(p. 140).

Another staff member recorded her feelings:

> Never felt so bad in all my time in work with old people. At tea there was only
> one other member of staff on. Mr Fothergill went out of tea, there was diarrhoea
> everywhere. Then Mr McNab slumped down in his chair, Mr Peat was ill, Mr
> Gasden said he couldn't sit there and watch Mr McNab eat, Mr Stevens was in the
> sitting area, spitting away, refusing to leave though three people were eating their
> tea in there. (p. 240)

Ward (1996) writes that working in therapeutic communities for
children and young people,

> like other forms of focused professional helping, makes strong demands upon our
> personal energy, commitment and morale, and if we are to invest of ourselves so
> greatly, we need to learn how to do so without totally depleting or even destroying
> ourselves in the process. We need to learn how to sit close to the deepest pain –
> which may involve confronting our own equivalent pain – and yet not to become
> crushed by it. We need to find ways of helping others to release their own restora-
> tive and therapeutic potential, and having done so today, we need to be ready to
> try again tomorrow. (p. 231)

All staff are involved in the lives of residents in that they help residents with certain tasks. The purposes of residential homes differ
markedly, and therefore the nature of the staff task and of the interaction
between staff and resident varies substantially. Menzies (1959), writing
about nursing, notes the significance for nurses of the experience:

> Nurses are confronted with the threat and the reality of suffering and death as few
> lay people are. Their work involves carrying out tasks which, by ordinary stan-
> dards, are distasteful, disgusting and frightening.

In all residential homes staff will be faced with residents' and their
relatives' emotions. The tendency to focus on loss and pain should not
lead us to forget the potential happiness, peace and fulfilment in residential life. A move to a residential home is likely to follow some sort
of crisis and people are faced with questions about self, identity, losses
in moving, the problems of adjustment, indeed, for older people in
particular, questions about life and death. Menzies (1959) shows that it
is easy to create defences to shut off such openness to others' feelings.
However, the energy put into maintaining the defences is counter-
productive to the work: to pretend that residents' feelings are not real,
indeed to try to jolly people along, does not allow residents to recognize and deal with their pain. Further, shutting off feelings creates
problems for staff who will be dissatisfied with the quality of their

experience. Yet if the pain of residents is not denied, it affects staff who are reminded of their own pain; thinking about the ways in which events have turned lives upside down for others is a reminder of what might happen to themselves.

The staff task

Many of the major themes for residential work today were identified 30 years ago by the Williams Committee (1967). The committee examined questions such as:

- What is the nature of residential work?
- Has it a professional base?
- Is there a coherent, common identity to residential work which crosses traditional service delivery boundaries homes for children, younger adults, older adults and so on?
- Is there a career in residential work?

On rereading the report I am impressed by the quality of the analysis and the pertinence to today. The report states that the staff 'have an extremely exacting task' but one that is 'also very rewarding'; the work 'needs special qualities both of mind and of heart' (p. 17). They note that there is 'limited understanding of the nature of the job or of the skill and responsibility involved' and that staff want recognition for their work (p. 24).

They examine the reasons why the task demands more than the skills and knowledge used by people in caring within families. The qualities or capacities staff need are stated as:

- 'a strong liking for their fellow human beings';
- 'compassion for those suffering from some misfortune or infirmity';
- 'insight and humility';
- 'energy and resourcefulness';
- capacity 'to take decisions when definite action is called for';
- 'serenity and a respect for others';
- 'knowledge of complex human personalities and relationships';
- knowledge of the way residents' behaviour 'has been fashioned by their lives, their families and their social backgrounds';
- 'technical skills of home-making' (pp. 32–3).

The report continues by identifying 'the necessity to get the co-operation of as many as possible of those living in the home in its running', to create 'amongst a number of people the feeling that they are living together rather than simply being "housed" together'.

However, residential work is not just about knowing what to do: it is concerned with finding ways to put that knowledge into effect and to bring about desired ends. For example, accepting the well-documented view that coherence among a staff team is a precondition for successful practice does not result in the coherence being created. The following extract makes the point in relation to residential child care:

> 'Residential work', the name for the practice that some of us have taught as a trade, is more than what staff do as a consequence of what they know about children and the reasons for their behaviour: it is about style and skills in being with children. Training for residential practice has the danger of leading to prescribed systems rather than allowing solutions to emerge. The same remains true for teacher training: would-be teachers have to learn about the ways in which children learn and the different means that are available to aid such learning. Further, they must learn about the details of management of children in groups, and the importance of the mechanics and the process of teaching as well as the knowledge of the subject. The recognition that the art of teaching can be learnt, however, should not lead to mechanistic adoption of certain techniques: nor should this happen in residential work. As I write, I have become more aware of the essential for good practice being the understanding of people (child, other adults and self) and the 'residential method' needs to follow from this. (Clough, 1997)

The nature of residential work

First, many staff tasks are carried out in front of other staff members or residents who, while not necessarily directly participating in the activity or even watching, will note what is happening. The work is semi-public and staff will be conscious of whether or not they themselves think they performed a task well.

Any number of my own experiences as a teacher and housemaster some 30 years ago in approved schools touch on this theme: supervising a meal with 80 young people, aware of the changes in noise and atmosphere, knowing that colleagues were eating their meal next door; looking after the residents in a break in the morning routine while staff had their coffee in a room that looked out over the yard; responding to individual young people while remaining responsible for and aware of the group of other young people; and so on.

Second, the staff task is carried out by a number of staff, a group or unit. They share in creating the conditions for work and in interaction with a particular resident even if a particular worker is designated as special or key worker. Beedell (1970) writes of 'the unit as worker'. It is imperative for successful practice that workers co-operate: they must examine differences between them, raise questions with each other about approach and work out procedures; they must not play out their disputes in their work with residents. As in families, tensions between staff members may be displayed in daily living events: in whether rooms are left tidy or the washing up done at the end of a shift; or in whether a staff member is helpful when another wants to negotiate when to help a resident take a bath. Further, again as in families, one worker may make differences with another apparent, even though overt statements of co-operation are made.

The work is peculiar also in that much of it can never be seen to be completed: what one worker does is carried on by another. Thus a care worker in a home for people with learning difficulties will see a resident return from a day out at a local centre, distressed by something that has happened. The worker will try to find sufficient space to be alongside this person while not ignoring the other residents; and, further, to provide space for the resident to discuss the matter without forcing such conversation, to show that the person's distress has been noticed and that what happens to the resident matters to the staff member. All of this may continue over several hours but at some stage the staff member finishes the shift and passes the work (and the resident) on to another person. This can be described as 'serial' work.

Interaction between worker and resident

Beedell (1996), commenting on staff–resident interaction in residential child care, states that the word 'relationship' 'easily becomes a debased currency and meaningless'.

> After much searching of mind and heart I had come to a definition of a 'good' relationship which rested on two elements of: a) the possibility of comparatively less defended interaction, and b) mutual recognition of the parties 'actual and potential *value and threat* to one another'. (p. 263, original italics)

What is, or what should be, the relationship between worker and resident? 'Do you behave like a hospital matron, a hotel manageress or a devoted daughter?' asked one head of home in Townsend's study over 30 years ago (1962, p. 147). Questions of the same type can be asked today for care staff in homes for adults. I have listed various options:

Is currently the relationship between resident and staff member that of:

a) mistress or master to servant;

b) guest to hotel staff;

c) individual to caring relative;

d) tenant to landlord/landlady?

Or should the relationship be one of these? There are other ways of looking at the same question, for example in terms of a model that recognizes the deficits of the resident (that is the inability to do certain things) and sees the staff member as the equivalent of a pair of hands to do those things. (Clough, 1998a, p. 19)

It is essential to remember that any definition needs to take account of the fact that there is a task to be undertaken and there is a relationship to be established.

Thus, if the model is constructed on the basis that people who cannot manage certain activities need someone else to help them undertake that task, the relationship between these two people might be defined as:

the resident as employer ('I have this task which I want you to do for me');

the resident as in receipt of a gift: the assistant has assumed control because of the nature of giving. (Clough, 1998a, p. 19)

Models which see adult residents as consumers who should be able to purchase and control service provision, fail to take account of the reality that residents may be frail and unable to define how they want services or to oversee their production.

Sinclair *et al.* (1988) interviewed numbers of people who received services of home care, occupational therapy and social work. The examples from care in a person's own home provide useful clues to understanding something of the complexity of direct care. They found that the benefits brought by home helps were both practical and social (p. 95). There are other aspects of the relationship that are interesting: clients appreciated thorough work but, while they wanted things done 'their way', did not always find it easy to ask for what they wanted; there was a reluctance to give orders.

There are writers such as Morris (1993) in the field of physical disability who put the case for individuals who need services to be getting them as citizens with rights who will then take responsibility for the management of the service: they will hire and fire staff, pay them with money received from social security and negotiate terms. Such models give the user authority and power, and they remove the stigma of being dependent. But they fail to reflect the difficulty that many people have in negotiating with workers for the services they want, difficulties which are compounded when the person is frail, feels dependent or is not always competent to manage the transactions. My point is not that such models are inappropriate: rather that they have a key element but miss out on others.

The more that residents need help with daily activities, the more important is the interaction between staff member and resident: the language staff use to talk to residents, their manner when undertaking residents' intimate physical care and the amount of time which they make available are all significant variables over which the staff member has considerable control.

Resident/resident interaction

Staff who undertake tasks for and with residents are of great importance in residents' lives. But, as Counsel and Care (1995) state:

> Writing about residential care has focused on the duties of staff; we can easily ignore the relationships which exist between residents, the responsibility residents are willing to assume for each other, and the mutual benefits from such interactions.

> A resident... had visited a close friend in the home and held her hand when 'she knew she was going'; the friend in due course died 'quietly and gracefully, with no fear or horror'. As a result of this incident and of witnessing the care given to other very sick residents, this lady said she was 'not in the least afraid of dying'. (p. 15)

There is a danger that environments are created in which residents' involvement with other residents is circumscribed.

Motivation of workers

If the job is as complex and demanding as I suggest, the question emerges as to the reasons why people might want to do it. Consideration of motivation is important but full of pitfalls. Many workers will speak of 'a wish to help others', a notion that at times has been derided as naive. Yet a fundamental aspect is, or should be, a concern for others. The wish to help or the concern for others has to be tempered with knowledge of what the job is and what is to be expected.

Many staff in a study of a home for older people said that they wanted to make residents happy (Clough, 1981). Others commented that they were rewarded when residents thanked them. Both of these comments have elements which are appropriate and elements which have the danger of distorting the work or demotivating the staff member. Some residents, in spite of best endeavours, may not be happy. They may be overwhelmed by losses they have endured, their disturbance, or their confused picture of their own worth. The problem with wanting residents to be happy is that if they are not, it may seem to staff like personal failure. In such circumstances staff may exert considerable pressure on a resident to do things which are thought to be 'for their good'. They are to be made better in spite of themselves. There may be increased control or interference by staff in residents' lives. There is a fine line for a staff member between appropriately testing whether a resident wants to join in with an activity or creating an expectation, informal but nevertheless powerful, that staff prefer it if residents do not stay in their rooms.

Wanting gratitude has parallel dangers: residents who do not show gratitude may be labelled as ungrateful or given less attention. Staff may feel undermined in that they are not getting the rewards they expect from the job.

What is important is that the wishes to help or to be thanked are recognized as legitimate and as feelings that are within all of us. However, the measure of satisfaction must be against the reality of the task and against a picture of 'a good day's work'. The test is not that of gratitude.

Over 35 years ago, Monsky (1963) conducted a study of work in residential child care. The respondents, primarily women, said that the job was more difficult than expected, demanding long days and a lot of domestic work. Monsky notes that one of the factors making it more likely that staff would stay in residential work was 'if they had previously been in jobs involving long hours on their feet'! However, the respondents stated that the job satisfied their maternal instincts and their need to give. An analysis today would have very different responses!

Motivation for residential work touches directly on our and others' understandings of self. I started residential work in the days when staff were expected to live on the premises. One of the views held of residential workers was that they were people who were in some way inadequate for they needed the protection or support of the residential establishment. I would have fiercely resisted such a statement. The presumption in the 1970s was that staff would be fuller people if they lived off the premises, developed their own lives and were less involved in the lives of the residents. Yet there may be a healthy wish to be a part of a community, perhaps to mix aspects of life and work.

One officer in charge of a home for older people commented to me how hard she found it now that she was no longer so involved in the life of the home. She slept on the premises but would no longer be woken if someone was seriously ill. Another was in charge of a very small children's home. The rooms she lived in with her husband were open to the children who shared many of their leisure activities. The presumption of the management was that she was too involved. Yet, today, this would be the model of what might be expected from fostering.

Another example comes from a different culture, a prospective residential worker in Japan today. She was taking an MA in social work. Her first choice of job was as a social worker in a residential home for older people. However, the function of a social worker in a Japanese residential home primarily related to management of the interface between external and internal worlds, such as an older person moving into a home. She had decided to work in a home for adults with physical disabilities because she wanted more contact with residents in their daily lives, which seemed to me a reasoned and appropriate decision. But some people making such a choice might, improperly, be striving for a job where they could exercise control over residents.

Indeed, having mentioned earlier the demanding nature of the work it is essential to recognize that there is an attraction in working with people who are in part dependent or disturbed. A part of this attraction may lie in the potential to help or to heal, but this in turn has an element of power and control: others are in need of our services. This recognition may be disturbing for any of us as we face the question as to why we choose to work in the settings we do. As a staff member it is not wrong to get satisfactions from being in these situations. The test lies in the way in which staff manage themselves. One of the aspects of the job which is liked is the ability to undertake the actual interaction in ways in which the staff member has considerable control. Staff have their domain, however much they may be under pressure of time or other constraints.

Staff and indeed other residents have significant power over a resident, although that must not blind us to the fact that residents themselves have power as individuals and as a group. Inherent in the power is the potential for oppressive practice. An aspect of the power is the potential to impose one's own values and practices in day-to-day events. It is hard for staff to have their views and to work with others who may have divergent opinions. This raises the importance of staff becoming aware of their own values and assumptions.

Who are the staff?

It is impossible to be precise as to the numbers of people who work in residential care and nursing homes in the UK. The best estimates suggest that the total number is probably over 700,000. This figure is staggeringly high and means that at any one time about 1.2 per cent of the *total* population is employed in residential and nursing home care.

The Residential Forum (1998a, pp. 84–9) has listed information on staffing from different sources.

Table 2.1   Residential staff in local authority
social services departments in England, 1995

	Numbers of staff	%
Homes for older people	40,519	59.0
Homes for people with physical disabilities	1,653	2.4
Homes for people with learning disabilities	11,149	16.2
Homes for children with learning disabilities	2,619	3.8
Mental health homes	1,923	2.8
Community homes for children	10,788	15.7
Total	**68,651**	

N.B. These figures are taken from Residential Forum (1998a, p. 85).

Tables 2.1 and 2.2 show the proportion of residential staff employed by, first, local authorities and, second, all employers. In any sector, most staff are employed in work with adults, predominantly older people. Local authorities have a far larger proportion of their staff employed in residential child care (between 15.7 and 18 per cent depending on the source of the information) than do voluntary organizations (2.4 per cent) and the private sector (only 0.4 per cent).

Table 2.2   Numbers of residential workers in
England in 1995 – by employment sector

	Local authority		*Voluntary*		*Private*	
Residential child care	13,000	*18.0%*	2,000	*2.4%*	1,000	*0.4%*
Residential care of adults	59,000	*81.9%*	81,000	97.6%	245,000	*99.6%*

N.B. These figures are taken from Residential Forum (1998a, p. 86), with
'ancillary workers' excluded.

It is not surprising to find that the overwhelming proportion of staff
employed are women. This reflects the dominant understanding of the
task of tending as being women's work, and reflects the low status and
pay of the work. Further, 52 per cent of all staff employed in private
and voluntary sector homes for adults are part time, a figure that is
likely to be similar for local authority homes for adults.

Again, it is not surprising that a larger figure, 17 per cent, of
managers are men compared to the proportions in basic care, where the
figure drops to men being only 9 per cent of the total work group.

However, the figures are different in residential child care. In this
sector the activity has been more professionalized and the majority of
staff are seen as professional rather than manual.

Table 2.3   Percentages of men and women in the residential workforce

	% women	*% men*
Managers and supervisors	82.9	17.1
Nursing staff	90.5	9.5
Care assistants	91.3	8.7

N.B. These figures are taken from Residential Forum (1998a, p. 88).

Analysis is further complicated in that there is no standard description of the different tasks workers do in residential homes. It is possible
to classify work activities in different ways:

1.   managerial: non-managerial
2.   professional (however defined): non-professional
3.   physical care or tending (for example helping to bath or to get up):
     support work not with residents (for example cleaning or cooking)
4.   physical care or tending (as above): other direct work with residents.

In the third category I am distinguishing people who work with residents from those who do not. The final grouping separates different types of direct care with residents: in the first, the core of the activity is the physical care; in the second, the work is more about talking and negotiating, setting of boundaries, support and development. The worker in residential child care will focus far more on this last category.

Of course the boundaries that are used in creating categories like this are artificial. Thus, some people's work is predominantly direct care with residents but involves some support work, and vice versa. This raises questions about job demarcation: how far should workers cross this type of boundary and what are the implications for training and pay?

Training and qualification

The workforce is largely unqualified. The precise meaning of any such statement in relation to residential care needs careful checking because there is no agreement as to what is the appropriate training and qualification. Some people may have qualifications but these may not be regarded as sufficient for the activity of residential care. Many commentators would now agree that neither nurse training (the most common qualification held by those working with adults in residential care) nor social work training are sufficient on their own for the task of direct care.

> In residential homes, however, where the primary purpose is the provision of a living environment, the skills of social care come to the fore in taking a more holistic view of the lives of residents and a much greater emphasis has to be placed on their control of their own lives. In this setting, therefore, the skills of nursing are relevant but not sufficient on their own, and some systems used in hospital need to be positively unlearnt by nurses working in homes. (Residential Forum, 1998a, p. 60)

Twenty-five years ago Tizard (1975, pp. 62–4) argued that managers of units for children with learning disabilities were affected by their professional training: those who had been nurse trained had lower rates of interaction with children than those who had been child care trained. (The full study is reported in King *et al.*, 1971.)

No other country has tried to create a cohesive identity around residential work, although some have residential workers highly regarded as specialists in child psychiatry. For example, a *psycho-éducateur* is a person who uses psychiatric expertise in the setting of a special school or home.

The arguments for creating different work identities take various forms. One is that residential child care should ally with related child care professions as part of a new 'child care expert' profession, perhaps with similarities to the *psycho-éducateur* model. A second is that there should be a realignment around direct care, the activity undertaken by those who provide some aspects of direct physical care to those whether in their own homes, day centres or residential homes (Clough, 1997). Third, without establishing the professional base for practice, are those who argue that residential work should be split from social work with training based around National Vocational Qualifications/ Scottish National Vocational Qualifications (NVQ/SNVQ) competences. There is little argument from within residential work for maintaining the links with social work.

The real danger in the UK is that residential workers are rarely seen as *specialists*: they may be thought of as devoted, patient and so on, but not often as experts in assessment and intervention.

We have to recognize also that the claims for training remain largely in the realm of what I term the 'hopes and dreams' from training (Clough, 1997). Barr (1987), in an excellent summary of reports on training, writes:

> Taken together, *the benefits attributed to training* in the reports add up to a package which holds the potential to improve practice. If staff of better calibre, with benefit of training become more competent, less isolated, enjoy better status and morale and can see more career prospects, cope better with stress and feel that they are being helped to develop as people, then high rates of staff turnover should fall... Staff relations will be more lasting, paving the way for better teamwork. Relations with residents will also be more lasting and this, combined with the greater experience and training of staff, should pave the way for better assessment, planning and monitoring of care for the resident as an individual. In that context, behavioural problems should also be more manageable. (p. 53) (My italics)

I contend that training is an imperative for staff at all levels in residential care practice. I have never met anyone who lives in a residential home or has a relative in a home, who is not horrified that most workers have no training of any kind. Alongside this we need research to examine the effectiveness of training.

Today there are far more common elements than formerly in the training of different professions. Most include human development, sociology and psychology together with skills in communication. In reviewing training for residential work, accreditation of prior learning needs to be approved for such common elements. This would allow the construction of additional modules and would not devalue former learning.

The practice of residential work

Given the uncertainties discussed above, it may seem strange to produce a book focusing on the genericism of residential work. Yet we cannot wait until there is a resolution to the debate as to the skills for practice, the professional base, the training and the career routes. I have no doubt that there are core aspects of living and working in residential homes that demand from staff a theoretical base (that is a framework for knowledge and understanding), sound ethical principles and practice skills. This cluster of knowledge, skills and values is needed in all homes, but not all staff will need the same depth of knowledge or skill. What is essential is that the cluster is available within the workplace and this may be what others mean when they write of 'a competent workplace' (Pottage and Evans, 1994).

Certainly, it is imperative not to force a mould on all residential work: there are differences in task and, consequently, in knowledge, skills and training.

An environment in which staff can work well

King *et al.* (1971) compared different types of units in terms of outcome for the lives of children with learning disabilities, describing some as 'child orientated' and others as 'institution orientated'. They made comparisons, for example, on degrees of block treatment (getting everyone to do the same thing at the same time), rigidity of routine, social distance between staff and children and the extent to which there was coherence between the worlds of staff and children. This largely sociological attempt to understand what affects the daily lives of residents is developed in the extensive work of the Dartington Social Research Unit's studies of residential child care.

Tizard (1975, pp. 59–62), commenting on the 1971 study, argued that, in the units where heads were given more responsibility, there were measurable differences in children's behaviour: they were talked to more, rejected less, were more likely to be alongside staff when staff were doing jobs and did more things for themselves. Moreover, the impact on senior staff of having more responsibility affected junior staff who also treated children differently; further, in the places where heads had more authority there was also less job demarcation.

The ideas are central to an understanding of daily life in residential homes. The regime in which staff work and, in particular, the nature of the authority given to the head of unit, has a significant impact on the lives of residents.

Menzies-Lyth (1988) has given particular attention to the relationship between the organization of tasks and the authority and responsibility accorded to staff. She contends:

> Thus, in considering adults as models, one would give attention to maximizing the opportunity for them to deploy their capacities effectively and to be seen by the children to do so. Indeed, one may go further: experience has shown that in a well-managed institution for children, the adults as well as the children actually gain in ego strength and mature in other ways. The adults thus provide better models. (p. 2)

She describes the way in which food was managed in one establishment to which she was consultant: the matron (it was some time ago as the title indicates) ordered the food for individual house units; the house-mothers thought that there was not enough food and took little responsibility for managing the arrangements; the children blamed the house-mothers for inadequate food; house-mothers explained to the children that it was not their fault – the problem was the matron. The system was changed. The house-mothers were given the authority to order the food and assumed the responsibility to ensure that the arrangements worked satisfactorily; in turn, the young people took greater responsibility for their own use and management of the food that was available.

This is similar to a comment that heads of homes for adults in local authorities used to voice: they complained that they were required to buy certain household articles from central suppliers. 'Give us the money', they would argue, 'and we can use it better.' Indeed, one of the main reasons given by some local authority managers who moved to run private establishments was that they would be able to have greater control of the way in which they ran their establishments.

Literature written about therapeutic communities emphasizes the need to maximize staff and resident potential. It is asserted, correctly in my view, that residents will not be able to achieve their potential and gain maximum control and responsibility for their lives, unless staff have maximum, appropriate responsibility for their work. If it is accepted that both staff and residents have potential to contribute to the life of an establishment and to the furtherance of the primary task, then the means to tap into such potential have to be sought. The therapeutic community approach to work with adults did this explicitly. Rapoport's (1960) review of Maxwell Jones' pioneering work at the Belmont Hospital noted that the total social organization rather than the doctor alone was seen as affecting outcome. Four central aspects of the 'therapeutic community approach' were described: democratization, permissiveness, communalism, and reality confrontation. The patients were to take an active part, all members were to show tolerance, there was to be 'a tight knit and inter communicative set of relationships' and patients were to be presented with interpretations of their behaviour (p. 54).

Early writing on residential work has parallels with later writing on management in recognizing that there needs to be agreement between stakeholders as to ends and means. In residential work there were expectations that there should be agreement on system maintenance and a way of living (Wolins, 1974; Clough, 1982). In management literature there has been a focus on 'shared values', the idea being that if there is overall agreement on the values which underpin the organization, then staff may be given far more freedom in their work (Peters and Waterman, 1982; Clough, 1990).

To recap:

- many of the key events in residents' lives are those which take place with face workers on numerous occasions through the day;

- the way staff behave to residents, in effect how they manage themselves and the events, has a significant impact on residents' lives, potentially on residents' feelings about self;

- no guidelines or systems of control can create staff who will behave appropriately – we all know what it is like when workers in other settings relate to us with learnt behaviour, perhaps particular styles of telephone response;

- staff have considerable scope in what they do and say in the frequent interactions with residents;

- staff will manage these events best in line with the goals of the organization if they are given the maximum appropriate responsibility and authority.

In training for residential work, frequently I have begun with an attempt to encourage staff to remember what they thought about residential life when they first started work, in particular what they imagined it must be like to be a resident. Menzies (1959) contends that attempts to push feelings aside by the creation of work patterns and systems are counter-productive to the task.

It is also essential to capitalize on staff potential in terms of creativity. Again this matches attempts in industry to build on the understandings which staff doing the work have of the ways in which improvements could be made to production. Staff in residential work frequently consider that they have no opportunity to contribute their ideas: in part this may be that they think their ideas are not valued; in part that there is no space to put them forward. The task for managers is to create an environment in which such ideas are discussed and to involve staff in the life of the establishment.

As a student I was asked on a short placement to write a report on the working of the laundry at Dingleton Hospital, which was just developing as a therapeutic community. As with many other mental illness hospitals at that time, some patients worked in the laundry. In the wards much effort was being put in to establish systems to ensure that all staff and residents were involved. The principal means of achieving this was through a community meeting. The laundry seemed to me an area which was excluded from this: staff were isolated, had no clear understanding as to the new purpose of the hospital and did not see themselves as playing any part in it. As a consequence, the patients in the laundry were treated as they had been formerly: as hands to process the work.

Creating a climate in which staff can work well will be pursued in later chapters on management, but must include supervision of people's work.

Selection

Much of the recent focus on selection of staff has come from the realization that staff have abused residents in all types of residential homes. An immediate question follows: is it possible to exclude people who should not work in residential care? The answer is that better selection would debar most but not all. However, there are more positive reasons to assert the importance of selecting the best staff. For all the reasons discussed above, staff play a central part in the lives of residents and it is imperative that the people employed are those who are the most rounded, and will not meet their own needs at the cost of residents. This statement recognizes that people, properly, want satisfaction from their work and have their own needs. The discussion earlier on motivation recognized that this is not inappropriate. But it is wrong if it is the interests of the worker that drive the interaction with residents.

Perhaps at the heart of good selection is to find staff who *like residents*. Any such phrase needs qualification because it is not meant to imply a cosy or patronizing approach. The test of how prospective staff regard residents is fundamental. This should be linked to two other factors: the way the person gets on with other adults with whom they will be working and their maturity in terms of understanding of self.

Beedell compiled a list of attributes for residential work with children and young people (Beedell and Clough, 1992, pp. 11–13). The precise listing would need to be adapted for different jobs and varying types of residential home.

Is the person:

Concerned for children and young people?

Does he or she *like* them?

Can they play and be comfortably alongside children?

Are they, at core, independent enough to withstand the batterings of children who are at the least adrift and may be very damaged and bewildered?

Can they serve as reasonable role models?

Can they relate to adults as well as children?

Negatively, are they themselves dependent on a structure, or a reliving of childhood or a romantic, idealized world of childhood?

He proceeded to ask whether the person was '"put together"... intelligent... enough to see the complexity of social interactions... , had adult skills outside child care... could be administratively responsible... ', and was open to support. From this he stressed the importance of trying to understand the person's 'deep level motivation' and 'sexual maturity', recognizing that both are complex areas.

In selection it is imperative that there is clarity about the nature of the task and the core capacities that are wanted. Once these are specified, it is necessary to look at the mechanics for selection, being aware

that candidates are not always truthful and that some terrible appointment mistakes have been made when set procedures have been ignored.
The following should be standard for all appointments:

- providing candidates with core information about the home;
- producing a job description and person specification;
- asking for written references, including from the previous employer
  and from the last social care employer;
- checking with referees; (there are examples of staff fabricating
  references);
- checking the qualifications listed by candidates;
- time for the candidate to visit the home, meet residents and staff;
- interviewing;
- the appointment should be for a trial period.

In the future it is likely that some of the checks will be undertaken
through examining the person's status with the newly established
General Social Services Council. For certain posts there will also be
police checks to be undertaken. Some employers may argue that such
proposals are impractical: they contend that the procedures take too
long and are not necessary for part-time staff. There are too many
examples of people being dismissed from one home and starting work
at another for such casualness to be acceptable. In homes where there is
a comparatively high staff turnover it may be worth employers establishing a bank of staff who have been appointed through set procedures.

Equality of opportunity

The way in which procedures are carried out will tell the candidates much
about the home. Any of us can recognize organizations which go through
the motions of following set procedures but do not appear to practise
them. Nowhere is this more likely than with equal opportunities policies.
On the one hand such policies can be integral to the life of the home; on
the other hand they be little more than glib statements. It is essential that
everybody has confidence in the integrity of the appointments system, so
correctness in advertising and procedure is essential.

> The test [of an equal opportunities policy] is found in everyday events: who does
> the washing up, mends clothes, cooks, makes decisions? Has anybody understood
> why someone cares about what she or he eats or wears, and has anyone ensured

that understanding is translated into action? Is it accepted that dismissive stereotyping which reinforces the very low self-esteem of so many residents does
continuing damage? (Beedell and Clough, 1992, p. 15)

The implications of equal opportunities for staffing and appointments
will need to be examined for different homes. Young people in homes are
more likely than the population at large to have poor experiences of
parenting, often with one parent, usually the father, absent or uninvolved.
The relationship of men to women in the residential home therefore is of
great significance. Staff in homes for young people do serve as role
models, and therefore must be representative of ethnicity and culture.

In homes for adults, staff are not role models, although their style of
interaction will have immense impact on the climate in the home.
Consideration has to be given in appointments to ensuring that the staff
group as a whole has inside understanding of the experiences of residents. Patterns of employment should be examined: are women, people
from ethnic minority groupings or those with disabilities overrepre-
sented at some levels and under-represented at others?

Structures

Much of the focus of this chapter has been on the ways in which in an
organization which runs a residential home there needs to be understanding of the activity of residential care and procedures to appoint the
best staff. Yet such internal systems are influenced by external structures and it is fitting to end this chapter with the reminder of that.

If, as I argue, the quality of staff has a dramatic impact on the lives of
the people who live in residential homes, then we have to consider the
attractiveness of the work. Like nursing, the role of tending others has
been seen as 'women's work'. It holds low status. Care assistant pay in
homes for adults is around the level of the minimum wage. The
rewards for some have been in flexibility of hours and ability to work
part time. Levels of pay in residential child care have risen substantially over the last 15 years and are now similar to those in nursing,
teaching and social work.

There is recognition by many people of the importance of the activity
of direct care. They want to play a part in providing good care. The
impact of training and of careers in direct care cost money and, consequently, are in direct conflict with assertions of market principles that
want purchasers of residential care to reduce charges for care. Even if

part of the costs of training are borne by staff themselves, as the Residential Forum (1998a) suggests, the changes proposed cannot be achieved without additional funds. Some of the 'costs' of residential care are paid by staff on low wages in residential homes for adults.

In residential care the services provided are predominantly services provided by people. A nurses' leader, in presenting her case for nurses to get better rates of pay, on the day that I am writing this, has argued that managers want to make a false comparison between providing facilities and paying better wages. 'If you don't have the nurses', she argued, 'you don't have the services' (Hancock, 1998).

3

Direct Care: Task, Theory and Context

In a home for adults with learning disabilities, a residents' meeting is taking place. This takes place once a fortnight, and is chaired by one of the residents. When the meetings were first held, staff dominated both the setting of the agenda and the discussion. This has changed and residents play a major part in the life of the meeting, although staff still participate directly themselves and help some of the residents to join in.

Topics of discussion in recent meetings have included: the proposals of the organization which runs the home to develop more special housing and to reduce the number of residential homes; residents' concerns about one of the group who has been very disruptive at several formal events at which outsiders have been present; planning a party for someone who is leaving; preparation for a new resident to move in; the run down condition of the downstairs lavatories; a report from a recent inspection visit.

Perspectives on residential living

The discussion at the meeting of the plans to develop more special housing raises an inevitable question as to the future of this particular home and residential care in general. Not surprisingly some residents will wonder whether they would be happier in their current home or one of the new special housing units. What has been their experience? How are they to compare the community where they live with the new unit?

Some of the apprehension and ambivalence towards residential homes has been examined in Chapter 1. How does this affect the lives of residents and staff?

It is impossible to state with any certainty that residential homes came into being to achieve a particular aim. Establishments for children in fact always fulfilled various functions: they did offer education and training; they provided housing and protection; they also removed from the streets young people who appeared to pose a threat. The same was true for the large mental illness hospitals: they offered asylum; they contained; and they treated. The function of removing people who were problems and making them less visible was particularly noticeable with mental illness hospitals where, around cities like London, the hospitals were built in a belt outside the town.

It is essential to recognize this mix of function. Accounts which emphasize just one aspect miss the confusion which may even have been part of the attraction of residential homes: they could be seen as places which were offering improved prospects while they contained people who seemed a threat.

> The rescue movement was driven forward by a mixture of motives and incentives that may be broadly characterized as social insecurity, missionary zeal, and economic opportunity. (Parker, 1988, p. 25)

Today the functions are even more confused. For example, one part of the critique of residential homes has recognized the damage that is done when residents are isolated from family and local community. The outcome has been a move to place residential establishments in the places where everybody else lives, alongside ordinary housing. Immediately underlying problems are brought to the surface as people ask questions such as: 'Do we want these people in our community?' 'Will they threaten our way of life?' Such feelings are obvious with young people because their troubled or troublesome behaviour may affect those who live nearby. But the same type of questions occur with adults. People may be uneasy at the prospect of a number of adults with learning disabilities living alongside them, not only because they conceive some aspect of their behaviour as a threat but because people's perceived difference makes others uncomfortable. Institutions that were set apart from the places people lived, protected from such discomfort.

A related factor is that there may be competing objectives, for example keeping people near their family may be in conflict with a wish to find a specialist establishment.

Having a residential home in the community also faces us more directly with dilemmas about other people's lives. A residential home exists because of the recognition by people in society of the need for provision or intervention. The problems inherent in that intervention may have been hidden when homes were more isolated. For example, there is a widespread expectation that residential homes for older people will look after residents, a notion that seems to involve keeping people safe. Alongside this are expectations that older people will be able to exercise choice and be cared for with dignity. What then is to happen if the residents walk out of the home, which is an open establishment, and are thought to run the risk of an accident, to be neglectful of self (perhaps walking outside in night attire) or a nuisance? The fact of living in a residential home has changed the perception of problem and responsibility: when living in one's own home such behaviour involved interaction and negotiation between the individual and others, perhaps neighbours or police. The move to a residential home has involved the staff and managers of the home in just such dilemmas.

Reports into life in residential homes through the twentieth century have examined what happens within homes in comparison with what happens outside. In terms of residential establishments for children, people have asked both whether the lifestyle is satisfactory and whether it is likely to equip children to manage when they leave the home. In the 1920s and 30s reports from the chief inspectors of reformatory and industrial schools stressed these points:

> Doubts were expressed about the value of compulsory church: 'We wonder if boys of 16–18, marched to church on a Sunday afternoon, will attend public worship anywhere after leaving the school.'   .

> The reports also offered advice on the dangers of over-protection, on putting too much emphasis on cleanliness, on encouraging visitors to see what went on and on fitting a boy for life. 'The man who finds his boys who are on licence to be spendthrift will realize that his refusal to allow them to handle money while in the school left them to learn its value, with deplorable results, in later life.' (Clough, 1970, p. 107)

Indeed, in evidence to a departmental committee in 1896, one witness stated:

> As a rule when they get into the world they seem altogether different from other boys. They are brought up in a certain mechanical way; they have always been supervised in every little thing they have had to do; they have used their judgement scarcely in anything... They are superintended all the time they are working, so that when they get out into the world... they seem about lost. (Cited in Clough, 1970, p. 83)

Today it is argued that residential establishments in the main do well in holding young people and helping them to manage themselves appropriately within the home or school: it is far more difficult to ensure that there will be a carry-over of these gains when the young person leaves (Bullock *et al.*, 1993). Thus there has been much written about training young people for independence.

Residential homes fulfil functions for society and exist within the structures, expectations and demands of society. To think about life and work in residential homes without recognizing the way in which external factors influence their use will lead to distortion. In particular, separating residential homes from their context results in a simplistic picture of life within the home, one in which it would appear that staff have the responsibility for practice and are to be held responsible for what happens.

Staff do have an immense impact on the lives of residents. They do have responsibility for the ways in which they work. But they work in homes which themselves fulfil functions for society and are influenced by that society.

Residential homes also fulfil a function for other welfare services: schools may pass on young people with whom they could not cope; housing facilities may exclude certain people because there is somewhere else for them to go; hospitals want to move people out to free their beds; social services need a base in which the young people can plan for fostering and to which they can return if the fostering fails.

Parker (1988, p. 3) writes that 'no informed conclusion about the future of residential care can be reached without paying careful attention to the kinds of external changes that are likely to determine its scale and character'. He continues:

> That, in turn, cannot be done satisfactorily without some understanding and appreciation of those forces that have shaped its history. The most important of these are located within prevailing social and economic structures.

He goes on to chart the correlation between the development of institutions and social regulation or control. The institutions, the large, residential homes of the nineteenth and part of the twentieth century, played a part in the management of social problems in that they helped to contain a problem. For example, relief to the destitute was to be provided in certain places called workhouses: other outdoor relief was stopped; people were to be deterred from asking for help because of the nature of the workhouse; but minimal standards were to be provided. Residential homes have continued to perform social control functions, although the nature of the control varies from place to place.

Many nineteenth-century institutions aimed to improve people: young people were trained for work in domestic service, agriculture and sometimes a wider variety of occupations. Certain establishments for adults also included work-like activities: these might involve training and varied in the sort of work which people were asked to do. At its worst, residents were doing repetitive, factory type jobs for minimal pay. A 1923 report on reformatory and industrial schools noted that 'children of school age had been employed on uneducative employment such as paper bag making and wood chopping' (Clough, 1970). Debates continue as to whether the work provided for residents was for their own benefit or to produce workers for trades which found it difficult to get employees.

Parker (1988) traces relationships between residential care and other social services: the establishment of a social security system; the changing organization of welfare services; the rising costs of residential care; the availability of people to work as staff. He adds a further dimension, changes to 'the environment of ideas'.

> One powerful nineteenth-century conviction, born of middle-class prosperity, self-confidence and optimism, was that behaviour could be altered and improved. This might be achieved through systems of coercion and inducement but quite as readily, and probably better, by training and treatment. (p. 7)

The fact of residence was being seen and used as a positive, an opportunity to allow staff to influence the lives of residents.

We have already seen that today, in general, people do not want to move into residential homes. The extent to which in the past residents of homes themselves wanted to live in homes cannot easily be gauged. However, we know that many people thought that residential homes were good ways of *both* controlling *and* looking after others.

What I am arguing is that today *the image* of residential life is negative and that this has an impact on those who live and work in homes. There is little of the earlier optimism that residential homes were places to help residents live well. I am not claiming that residential life is harmful: indeed, ways in which residential homes can be life enhancing is one of the central themes pursued in this book. Nevertheless *the persistent image* of residential homes remains, summarized by Parker in 1988.

> The idea of institutional life has always been viewed with repugnance by a broad section of the population. This attitude has persisted despite many changes and improvements and although now it may be weakening, it nevertheless continues to be influential. Its survival has been assured by at least four forms of reinforcement: the deliberate cultivation of a repellent image; reported cases of the abuse of inmates; the enforced association and routine of institutional life, and the compulsion often associated with entry as well as with subsequent detention. (p. 8)

Readers will need to determine whether this is accurate as a picture of today's residential homes. It is based in part on the folk memories of former huge institutions, the images of workhouse and orphanage. It is much rarer today for people directly to threaten others with a move to a residential home in terms such as, 'If you don't behave, you'll be sent away.' Yet, this is at times implied. Perhaps more significant now is people's realization that failure to cope may lead to a move from one's own home.

Any review of residential care must also take account of the fact that in some places the lifestyle imposed on residents has made them less able to cope. The earlier example from inspectors' reports claimed that young people were not able to manage when they left the home because they had not been allowed to manage enough of their lives when they were in the home. Forty years ago Barton (1959) described a condition, *institutional neurosis*, in which the person adopted styles of behaviour suited to institutional life. Such ideas, as those of Goffman which will be discussed later, are dismissed by some as being developed in very large institutions in a different age. Yet, today, we need to remain vigilant to the way in which the running of the residential home affects residents.

Most strategies for people who face problems stress that residential homes should be avoided whenever possible: thus guidance for children's services, compounded by oversimple interpretation of guidance, has emphasized children staying at home or in families; for young adults there has been emphasis on domestic style accommodation and measures of success for community care for older people have included a reduction in the numbers of places in residential homes.

The emphasis on living at home (or at least living in one's community) is founded on several building blocks:

1. the problems created by residential living;
2. an idealized view of family life;
3. a lumping together of all 'residential' establishments without taking account of differences;
4. the costs of residential provision.

First, it is true that sometimes residential homes have created their own sets of problems, but it is also true that homes have helped people to manage their lives, either through the support of physical care or through learning to manage their own problematic behaviour.

Second, it has been common to present a stereotypical picture of the poverty of residential life which is contrasted with a picture of perfect life in one's own home. The people who move into residential homes are likely to be those for whom one or both of these elements is lacking: either relationships with others have foundered or they cannot live as they would wish. In these circumstances a more adequate comparison is between life in a residential home in which there are gains as well as losses and life in one's own home in which there are losses as well as gains. I suggest that there is some truth for all residential homes in a statement that I have made about residential homes for older people:

> There are fallacies in the belief that for *all* people, at *all* times, living in the wider community is preferable. This stereotype is supported by a number of assumptions. The first of these places an idealized model of domiciliary care alongside a picture of inadequate residential care. (Clough, 1981, p. 11)

Third, the emphasis on the common features of residential living has allowed the huge differences between places to be ignored. Finally, the argument about costs has often been distorted. Residential care includes the costs of housing (including maintenance, heating, lighting), food, bedlinen, washing of clothes, personal care, leisure facilities and support or counselling. Comparisons are then made with the cost of *additional services* to someone in her or his own home, when many of the living expenses are excluded from the total because they are paid for in other ways. In this way there have been inaccurate comparisons of residential care of young people with fostering.

Knapp and Fenyo (1989) contend that there are expensive aspects to fostering which typically are excluded from costings: 'recruitment, selection, training and "matching" foster families with foster children'(p. 186). Further they argue that trying to recruit additional foster parents for hard to place children is not just adding on an average cost for each new foster parent: supply and demand will lead to additional costs in finding further foster parents; the costs of training and support are also likely to increase per foster parent.

> In common with a number of today's social care policy emphases, the encouragement of foster care as an alternative to residential care is based primarily on assumptions (and some evidence) about comparative effectiveness gauged in terms of client welfare, and reinforced by assumptions (but usually *no* evidence) about comparative costs. (p. 187)

They continue by claiming that the same arguments are used in making the case for the closure of long-stay hospitals, for domiciliary rather than residential care for older people or 'to substitute intermediate treatment for custodial sentences' (p. 187).

The combination of factors means it has been rare for residential homes to be regarded as valuable, specialist resources. In such an environment the creation of the desired positive perception of residential care is hard to achieve.

One further, distinctive aspect of residential life has an impact on people who live there: residents are living alongside others whom they are unlikely to know, whose interests they do not necessarily share and with whom they have not chosen to live. This is a peculiar situation for adults who, in their own homes, have become used to living with relatives or people whom they choose.

Differing perceptions on the task

The expectations of different groups may vary. Neighbours may presume that the staff of a children's home should stop children going out when it is judged that children should be kept in the home; official guidance makes clear that physical restraint, other than for a very short period, is not permissible. Except in the case of secure accommodation for children and young people, residents are free to leave a home if they choose. Staff are expected to face people with the consequences of leaving and perhaps to create ways in which residents will take time to consider their decision, but they are not allowed forcibly to detain people against their will. Thus, while staff may temporarily restrain a young person, they may not prevent the person leaving nor lock them in a room.

Similarly, adult residents have the right to leave a residential home. So, to lock doors in such a way that residents are unable to leave (whether directly locking a door to which a resident has no access to a key or through complex handles or locks) must be an infringement of a resident's liberty. Yet staff are expected to care for residents who may be thought to be a risk to themselves and possibly, although more unlikely, to others. Even the practice of electronic tagging of residents to monitor their leaving the home, raises questions as to legality. In terms of context it is essential that dilemmas of this sort are faced by management, staff, residents and their relatives: there is an uneasy collusion which avoids the problems and presumes that somehow the good practice of staff will sort out the problem. This is not fair on staff or residents. Residential homes operate in the context of societal expectations and of legislation, and the potential changes to laws on mental competence could have a significant impact on the lifestyle of residents and responsibilities of residential staff.

A study of functions allows examination of dominant beliefs. One current belief is that residential homes are better if they are smaller. This view is built on perceptive fragments which recognized the significant problems in many large residential establishments where the scale of the task often led to regimentation of residents. Yet very small places may have much less space for residents to be separate from others, may have fewer specialist facilities and reduce the number of people with whom residents can meet. Equally as important, one disturbed or disturbing resident can have a much larger impact on a small home. This is seen in many children's homes where, in a small home, it is harder to maintain the equilibrium faced with residents who become aware of the way in which their behaviour can dominate the life of the place.

This is not to argue for a return to larger homes: it is to question the certainty that a smaller home necessarily is better and it is to point to the way in which the dominant beliefs at any one time influence practice. They are a part of the context in which homes operate.

Authors have tried to categorize residential homes by type or function. For example, I have suggested that residential homes were thought necessary for three main reasons:

to carry out 'parenting' or 'tending';

to control residents;

to change behaviour. (Clough, 1982, p. 7)

Beedell (1970, p. 19) writes of three tasks in work with children: holding, nurturing and the development and maintenance of personal integrity. 'Holding' encompasses 'the customs and rituals designed to ensure the dependent child's survival and to protect him from danger, discomfort and distress'. 'Nurturing' relates to the development of social, physical and intellectual skills. Finally, 'the development and maintenance of personal integrity' refers to the 'social norms of individual development', and the ways in which children are helped to become 'whole people', as the term is understood.

The importance of approaches such as these which try to identify dominant characteristics in individual homes is that they allow comparison between places in terms both of ideological or theoretical framework and day-to-day practice. Debates about models tend to focus on whether the detail in any type is correct or whether a home fits neatly into any single category. The more significant dimension is to recognize that beliefs influence the way people work and live. So, models in residential care for younger adults could be based on different variables: for example, models of disability or housing management could be used. With children and young people, two key variables would be the dominant theoretical frameworks for interpreting children's behaviour and for determining how such behaviour is to be managed. The first variable faces staff with clarifying their response to the question, 'How do we understand the behaviour of these children?' The second posits a further question: 'What are the ways in which we are going to work?'

Thus the idea of models has at its heart that it should be possible to identify the key reasons for differences between places.

Another way to look at function is to consider the primary need of the resident:

1. is it for physical care on account of inability to manage various tasks of daily living? such inability may be directly physical (that is the person cannot get out of bed without assistance), may arise from an emotional state (mental ill health, confusion) or a combination of the two;
2. is it for assistance with the management of everyday life rather than the tasks of daily living? (that is people have not the capacity to plan and manage their relationships with the outside world and rely on the place and staff to assist with these);
3. is it for 'holding' and refuge? that is to establish boundaries for oneself and to one's behaviour, to find space to reflect, to recover past coping strategies or to learn new ones;
4. is it for a combination of holding and healing, whether because of disturbance or addiction?

Leat (1988, pp. 202, 215) in discussing residential care for younger physically disabled adults stresses the importance of being aware of similarities to and differences from other types of residential care: such homes are not concerned with curing, control or reform; the residents are permanent and it is the staff who are transient. She argues that it is reasonable to refer to places as 'homes' if the purpose is 'care' or 'development'.

But what does providing a home imply? Is home a place where one has rights, where one can be oneself or a place where one must give up individual rights in favour of collective comfort? The home philosophy may be used as a justification for allowing residents to stay out as late as they wish or as a justification for a single inflexible meal-time. (p. 215)

Residential care: the past and the future

Residential work has its roots in the past. Putting people together who were judged to face similar problems or to need similar treatment was a nineteenth-century mass solution to what was seen as a mass problem, in large measure a consequence of urbanization. These large establishments should be examined to understand how far they provided a better life than whatever else was available. In the twentieth century, the dominant move has been to try to humanize institutions, in part by considering the lifestyle of those who live in them, but predominantly by developing homes with far fewer residents. The forerunners of today's residential homes can be identified:

- almshouses;
- workhouses for adults and children;
- hospitals of different types, which were called at the time 'subnormality' or 'mental handicap', 'psychiatric' or 'mental' and 'geriatric';
- residential schools: (a) 'welfare type', including the reformatory, and industrial schools of the mid nineteenth century and the approved schools of the 1930s to 1970s; (b) progressive boarding schools, for example Summerhill established by A.S. Neill; (c) 'special' schools for different groups, such as those with physical disabilities, with learning difficulties or behavioural problems; (some of these were defined at one time as for pupils with 'emotional or behavioural difficulties', known as 'EBD');
- children's homes: the large, cottage-style homes of the late nineteenth century;
- children's communities, such as those of Homer Lane at Little Commonwealth;
- prisons and borstals; reformatory and approved schools, could be catalogued under a *treatment of young offenders* category as well as under the *schools* category above;
- therapeutic communities for adults: these developed from the work

of Maxwell Jones and others in the 1950s when they transformed large mental illness hospitals into therapeutic communities; some communities have focused on people with particular problems such as alcohol and drug abuse or mental illness.

More recently, the focus has shifted to ways in which places are integrated with local communities. The former institutions became total living environments, in which staff and residents could have all their needs met: housing, shopping, care, education and so on. The concern in today's language of 'social exclusion' has been that residents in particular and staff to a lesser extent were isolated, indeed deliberately set apart from others in the community. The development of small houses for people with learning disabilities typifies an approach in which people are to be included in their local communities. Yet, changing the buildings, essential as it is, does not guarantee inclusion: there are numerous examples of people in small homes having very little contact with neighbours and continuing to be isolated.

The boundaries of residential care and related work may shift.

Residential work: similarities to and differences from other tasks

Residential work involves functions akin to:

- housing provision and management
- nursing
- teaching
- field social work, including therapy or treatment
- home care
- day care
- hotel provision and management
- youth work
- occupational therapy
- physiotherapy
- fostering
- family care.

By this I mean that in residential homes there are aspects of the work that have some similarities with these other activities. It is not easy to define what it is that makes residential work distinctive from these.

Indeed, residential workers can be seen, whether by themselves or others, to be Jacks and Jills of all trades, masters and mistresses of none.

Residential homes differ from many other living arrangements in that typically residents do not own their rooms, are living apart from their families and have not chosen to live with particular people in the home. Further, residents are likely to be seen to have characteristics in common with other residents or to face similar problems.

Typically also, the staff are employed by the home owners or managers, not by the individual resident. The majority of care staff in work with adults are women. They are likely to be low paid and many have poor conditions of service. The job itself is physically and emotionally demanding.

The boundary which distinguishes a residential home from other housing styles is particularly difficult to define in relation to small homes. The boundary is in part linked to the definition for regulation purposes of a residential care home for adults:

> Any establishment which provides or is intended to provide whether for reward or not, residential accommodation with both board and personal care to persons in need of care by reason of old age, disablement, past or present dependence on alcohol or drugs, or present or past mental disorder. (Registered Homes Act, 1984)

Not surprisingly, consequent on such a definition, some places will wish to be defined as 'residential homes' for the perceived advantages, perhaps to attract custom, while others, to avoid requirements of the regulatory system that they believe inhibiting, may ensure their establishment is defined as housing or hotel rather than residential home.

Direct care

At the heart of residential life is the daily activity of nurturing and tending. In one way or another decisions are made as to the ways in which certain daily tasks will be carried out: getting up and going to bed, preparing and eating meals, washing up, washing and bathing or looking after clothes. There are some residential homes in which staff will aim to help residents understand themselves and their problems, perhaps also to set bounds on their behaviour. In all cases such objectives will only be realized if the foundation of good daily living has been established.

In residential work, house maintenance functions and direct care exist alongside each other. Parker (1981) uses the word 'tending' to describe the activity of physically looking after someone. Parsloe (1989, pp. 78–9) proposes that we should try 'to distinguish a person's needs in three areas, for accommodation, for tending and for affection'. She continues:

> So I am suggesting that people who are emotionally isolated, live in a group residence and are physically dependent, are likely to need accommodation, tending and affection. For those who have friends and relations, live in their own accommodation and are less physically dependent on those who tend them it is less crucial that there should be an emotional bond between them and those who tend them.

> Let me make it clear here that I am not suggesting that tending is ever adequate if it is done brusquely, without concern for a person's physical comfort and for their dignity. But it is possible to attend to someone gently and respectfully without liking or loving them for themselves, and it is possible for such attention to be acceptable to the person who receives it. Nor am I suggesting that loving ensures that tending is well done. Some aspects of tending need to be learnt, and some people need more tending than can be provided by those who love them.

The dilemma when attempting to analyse the task of residential work and determine the appropriate training is that good residential practice intertwines such direct care with an understanding of individuals. The care is provided in the context of a relationship of some type.

What may seem a mundane task, such as washing or bathing a resident, involves a number of activities: careful planning of the bathroom to ensure that there are appropriate aids but that the room does not become clinical and cold; consideration of the routine and regime of the home to allow flexibility so that residents may have a say in when baths take place; negotiation with individuals as to how they like to have a bath; thought as to how to minimize embarrassment in carrying out an intimate task for someone who is not one's intimate.

There may be particular problems that someone faces which make bathing difficult or worrying; or there may be physical conditions to which attention should be given at bath time. Further; there should be a consideration of 'who should bath whom?': does the sex or sexual orientation of resident and staff member have a bearing on such planning? There may be wider issues: negotiation with management or registration authority as to assessment of risk if people want to bath themselves or prefer bath water hotter than the maximum permitted by the guidelines.

Thus, the direct care should be personal and appropriate: for example, so far as possible, people should have baths in ways that suit their wants and needs and, indeed, should find the bathing to be a pleasurable experience. However questions of authority and control are immediately present: if a resident does not want to wash but is causing offence to other residents, what responsibility and power do staff or other residents have? Presumably this will differ in varying types of establishment.

The task described above is one of sensitive, physical care. Good residential work is embedded in such sensitive, direct care in numerous daily events: getting up, meals, washing and bathing, inbetween times (that is times when there are no scheduled activities), leisure pursuits, getting to the lavatory, and going to bed. It needs to be remembered that the residents are people who to a greater or lesser extent have found it difficult to manage some aspect of their daily living. Residential work demands that there is overall planning so that there is opportunity for the service to be personal. As most of us will know either from our experience of residential homes or other residential facilities such as hotels, it is easy for the demands of the system to mitigate against what we want as individuals. Good direct care is the bedrock of any residential home.

Thus, residential work has similarities with what people without training do in families, in particular parents with their children. However, there are tasks, methods and skills that can be learnt which are integral to residential work. Further, there are some features of 'being a resident' which are common to most homes, in particular the negotiation needed for the provision of services in situations where residents may have, or perceive they have, limited power.

Models for direct care

For most of us, our model of daily living and of intimate tending has been our own households and families, modified by other experiences. Thus we form views of the essentials in caring and of how to accomplish them from the households in which we were children, those in which we live with other adults in particular those who are our lovers and those in which we look after our own children. These have been powerful and formative: they hold memories of holding and comfort, pain and hurt; they are places in which we have blossomed and harboured resentments, been dependent and independent; in control and out of control, dependable and undependable. Inevitably the nurturing and tending of others (whether inside or outside households) are evocative of the ways in which we have been nurtured and tended, and, in turn, have ourselves nurtured and tended others.

The task of tending, whether as paid work or in a family, touches significant memories, good moments or barren experiences. Each individual staff member will feel more or less satisfied with their own lives. Particular aspects of their work will resonate with what has happened to them: perhaps specific tending tasks evoke memories of earlier experiences or the personality and characteristics of the person for whom the care is being provided remind the staff member of self or of others.

In addition, providing care for adults or children reminds us of potential problems in our own lives or in those of people whom we love: children who cannot cope, adults faced with disability, ill health and death. Tending is not an emotionally neutral activity. It may be that emotional distance (sometimes improperly thought of as a part of professionalism) is striven for, in Menzies' (1959) words 'as a defence against anxiety'. Being unwilling or unable to acknowledge the intensity of personal feelings in work does not make staff invulnerable: simply, it makes them differently vulnerable.

Direct care work requires staff to carry out these tending and nurturing tasks outside the normal familial setting. Intrinsically, this is neither easier nor harder but it is different in that we are caring for those who are not 'familiar', that is not part of our family. In direct care, the carer is carrying out the task as part of a job: there are no issues of kinship ties or family responsibility; at the end of the shift, the worker goes away knowing that the responsibility rests with somebody else. So it is reasonable to expect that the stress on the carer is reduced. The task of caring is not overwhelming and all-consuming in the way that it may be for a carer in a household.

For all staff in direct care there are traces, firmer or weaker, of the following:

- exposure to the pain and hurt of those living there;
- the potential to be touched or disturbed by the experiences of those for whom you are caring;
- a wish to do something to improve their lives, perhaps to heal and resolve;
- the need to get certain tasks completed: meals cooked and washed up; people helped with getting dressed or going to bed;

- tending tasks that may be physically demanding and unpleasant;
- tasks that having been done once will have to be done again and again: the person who has had a bath and enjoys feeling and looking good will get dirty and want another bath;
- uncertainty as to responsibility: for example should you leave alone or try to influence people who want to give up;
- the expectations of others (in particular relatives and the public) that certain types of control will be exerted: perhaps that adults will not be 'at risk' of having an accident or younger people not allowed to be a nuisance in the locality;
- the consequent issues of setting boundaries, stipulating and enforcing requirements, with the overarching aspects of power and control.

Thus there are a number of reasons why direct care workers may find the work difficult, may feel that the job is out of control, may have strong feelings roused, may get hurt both physically and emotionally and may relive past experiences. Tending is a complex and demanding task.

A theoretical base for direct care

Residential work has similarities with other activities but important differences, as the following extract argues in relation to residential child care:

> In direct care the worker has temporary responsibility for the child in a combina-
> tion of education, play and healing. It demands direct control and direct care
> which will vary with the age and needs of the children: washing and changing
> nappies; providing meals; oversight of going to bed. There is a further element
> which is hard to define: the combination of concern for the child and trying to
> create an environment which will help the child's development. This is a general
> task, that is one which is undertaken for all the children, and a specific one in that
> it is adapted to encourage a particular child, for example to persevere with home-
> work or to face a situation of which she/he is scared. (Clough, 1997, p. 3)

Direct care is an activity in our society which has low status. The first reason for this is that direct care work in informal settings, that is in families and households, tends to be thought of as unskilled. The second is that direct care as a job is low paid and it is common for people to state that they want to move out of such activity so that they can do something more skilful.

This places any attempt to examine the skill and theoretical base of direct care in a dilemma. Is it possible to assert both the importance and the skill of direct care work without overemphasizing, perhaps becoming pretentious, in the claims? The idea that direct care work should be planned and use skills can lead easily to a position where every interaction between people is weighed and calculated. Being conscious of the significance of the work should not result in such claims.

Similarity and difference between residential homes

A general book on residential work, such as this one, needs to convey both that there are features common to residential work and that there are substantial differences, first between types of homes and, second, between individual homes. It is like asserting that there is an activity called education but that schools differ in pupil intake, task and philosophy. It is essential early on to stress divergence.

The study of common factors in residential homes has tended to mask differences. Thus much of the theorizing about life in institutions has emerged from the study of very large residential establishments, often for several hundred people. The word 'residential' is used also to describe houses for three or even less people. It needs no imagination to realize that there are huge variations in these two extremes. The point becomes even more firmly emphasized when comparisons are made across countries. During the 1970s and 80s there was a programme of deinstitutionalization in Massachusetts. Young people were to be moved out of the institutions into other facilities in the community. This was held up as a mirror to the UK. In fact, in the main, the development in the USA was of a move from very large places into smaller residential establishments. By and large the UK establishments were smaller before the American experiment than were the American places afterwards.

Tizard *et al.* (1975) in an important study criticized what they termed *the steampress model* which looked for similarities between places and ended up forcing establishments into moulds.

> Most previous research on residential establishments and their functioning, has started, not from the obvious fact of institutional variety, but from the equally obvious fact that the members of any class of institutions tend to resemble each other. (p. 3)

In their book they had a number of researchers striving to understand the *differences* between residential homes. Why is it that one place differs from another? They examined four differentiating factors: ideological variation; organizational variation; staffing variation; and resident response. In organizational arrangements, they gave particular prominence to the extent to which autonomy led to improved performance by residents. They suggested that autonomy frees 'staff to make use of their own good qualities' (p. 9).

Current writing on residential child care has emphasized the importance of coherence between structures and culture (Brown *et al.*, 1998; Whitaker *et al.*, 1998).

The essential for residential workers is an understanding that good residential practice does not happen by chance. It is founded on an understanding of the residents and backed by reflection on the ways the residential home should operate. There needs to be general coherence between the varying stakeholders (residents, staff, managers, relatives, neighbours and others) but detailed agreement as to style and practice among the staff.

However, the identity of what we term 'residential work' is confused. For example, I have put forward a case for reinterpreting the functions of residential care for older people as 'housing plus care'.

> The core of the model is that the individual older person is seen as owner or tenant; thus, they live in their home which others may visit to provide services. This shift in designation makes a direct contractual difference first to the control and responsibility of the individual older person for the building and the life style within it and, second to the relationship between older person and those providing care services. (Clough, 1998a, p. 27)

Such an approach questions the existence of what is now called residential work. However, the direct care skills, currently practised in the best of residential homes, will be essential in such housing plus care. Thus the themes of this book have continuing relevance, for they relate to the ways in which we can construct the best environments for the housing and care of those citizens who need support in some parts of their lives.

In concluding this chapter I return to people's perception of residential homes. Living in a residential home is expensive. Therefore, if the cost is to be borne by the state, the state will wish to be assured of the appropriateness of the move. Since there is the potential for more requests for residential care than the state is prepared to fund or able to supply, some form of rationing is needed. It is in this territory that we face a key dilemma. The demand for residential care in part will be influenced by the extent to which potential users find the idea of residence attractive. If residential homes were to be seen as more attractive, perhaps as specialist resources, the demand would rise. We have to ask how far 'less eligibility' lives on in a new guise.

There is evidence that shows the use of residential homes changes with cost and availability. Early studies into residential homes for older people showed that it was difficult to assess the numbers of homes needed because when a home was built in their locality, more people wanted to use it: demand increased with local availability (Davies and Knapp, 1981). We know also, not surprisingly, that usage is influenced by payment systems: there was a dramatic increase in the numbers of places in private residential homes for adults in the 1980s when the government allowed those who received state financial support through supplementary benefit to move into a residential home without a test of need.

So there is a tension between wanting residential homes to be seen as good places and wanting to ensure that they are used in the way that the state demands. In residential child care the tensions are different. If parents were to ask for their child to be moved to a residential home, they might be seen as trying to shelve their responsibilities. There is an interesting comparison to be made with the attitudes towards those who send their children to boarding schools. There are examples such as that of the Harlesden Community Project in the 1970s when a residential home developed as a community resource and young people actually wanted to move in: the social services department struggled to know how to cope with the notion of a popular home that had to work to exclude (Harlesden Community Project, 1979).

It emerges from the examples that demand for residential homes is linked to numerous factors. Perhaps the most significant is that residential homes have been used to house and care for people in problematic circumstances. Thus, residential homes are likely to be regarded with unease: we do not want to be in the situations which might lead to residential life.

4

What Residential Workers Need to Know: Theory for Practice

At a staff meeting in a home for children and young people, discussion is taking place about two young people. This is part of regular practice in this home which aims to consider in some depth all the young people on a cyclical basis. All members of staff have been asked to come to the meeting having written down information on their contacts with the young person: what was the event? what was your role? what did the young person do? how did he/she appear to be managing in relation to self, other children and staff? what were your feelings? A discussion follows.

Introduction

The task of residential work is to create good environments in which people can live, environments which will allow and encourage the provision of good physical and emotional care. The nature of the environment, indeed the nature of the task, must be appropriate for the particular people who live in the home and must adapt to their changing needs and wants. It is easy to make such a statement but far harder to determine what are those needs and wants and how to construct appropriate living arrangements.

The format for the staff discussion in the example above has been developed from an idea of Dockar-Drysdale (1973) known as a *context profile*. She considered that it was essential to get the whole picture of a child, and so wanted to highlight all aspects of their lives, capacity as well as problem. In addition she thought that the feelings engendered in the worker might provide clues to interaction.

So a particular theoretical approach to an understanding of children, leads to a method for practice. Consequent on an attempt to understand people, as apparent in this staff meeting, staff and residents have to construct the arrangements for daily living. These have to be appropriate for the residents in general and then have to respond to thinking as to what will be best for individual children. Importantly, residential life provides an opportunity to intervene in different ways, for example by working directly with an individual or by changing the systems in the home.

An everyday event, such as a conversation between worker and individual, is both an ordinary event and, potentially, special. Talk of theory may seem inappropriate, even artificial, getting in the way of normal interaction and treating every encounter between people as of immense psychological significance. Yet the conversation between individual and worker is not just a casual event. It occurs in the context of specific events in people's lives. To do their jobs properly, staff should have a general understanding of people, and a specific understanding of the experience of being in a residential home. The same would be true for teachers and nurses in the settings of school and hospital.

In residential homes it is dangerous to rely on personal viewpoints. The job is not just common sense. Residential work differs from activities however similar they may seem when done informally within households. The most significant difference is that it is a formal activity, undertaken as a job. Individual workers may not do whatever they like. There has to be a search for the rationale: a willingness to question; an ability to explain.

Imagine a situation in a residential home in which a staff member is concerned about a resident. Such concerns are of many different types: residents may seem unhappy or disturbed; they may be annoying other residents or staff; perhaps they are doing nothing but lie in bed at every available opportunity, or compulsively repeating some action. Three key questions follow: what is the role and responsibility of the staff member? are there any explanations which help the resident or the worker to understand, or to search for an understanding, of such behaviour? finally, are there any clues as to whether certain actions and responses are likely to have a desired effect?

Practising with theory

Theorizing is the construction of explanations for events. Theories, if they are good, help people to understand and interpret what they see:

they suggest that there are some patterns, the knowledge of which aids understanding. They do not provide the answers for action, nor should they be used as if they do.

Theories are important in being able to explain practice to others. Yet we must remember that theories are contested: individuals and groups of individuals have to work out the theories that make best sense to them. The existence of a theory does not mean that it is 'true'.

There are further warnings about theories. It is imperative that they make sense to the people who use them: the temptation to claim expertise by spouting undigested theory is to be avoided. Second, if theories are to be of use in practice, they should be described in language that people can understand. Finally, it is essential that theory which is not understood should be questioned: there are frightening examples of people being uneasy with a practice that they see but being put off from questioning by the seeming competence of a supposed expert.

Equally important as the search for understanding is a similar active search for how to respond: 'Given what we understand of the current state of this person (their needs, wants and experiences) what is our best response in terms of systems and individual work?'

The knowledge, skills and values needed by individual staff working in direct care

The lack of an accepted model or framework for residential work helps to explain the problems which face residential work. The following, written about residential child care, has general applicability.

> Too often residential work is undertaken with no analysis of problems and no theoretical base for practice. The consequence is that staff may be ill equipped to do the job, and outsiders... have no framework for examining what goes on... Too many people have been sucked into questionable ideas by the charm or charisma of individual managers or heads of homes.
>
> In default of a theory, people tend to fall back on simplistic analogies: the warm, caring substitute mother, the nanny, the 'public' boarding schools... This mix of implicit assumptions leads to low public esteem. (Beedell and Clough, 1992, p. 1)

There have been regular, sometimes repeated debates, over the last 50 years as to the identity of residential work. At different times residential work has been considered:

- a specific task – residential care with children *or* younger adults *or* older adults;
- a generic activity, in which the common, shared factors between different types of residential work are thought to have more significance than differences;
- a branch of social work;
- a specialist part of other disciplines, such as child psychiatry and treatment.

'Is residential work to be seen as part of social work?' asked the Central Council for Education and Training in Social Work (CCETSW) in 1973. At that time CCETSW decided that residential workers and field workers should be trained on generic courses with a common qualification. Currently there is a question as to the appropriateness of that decision. In particular there are concerns that residential work may not have benefited in terms of either theoretical development or attracting staff from its links with social work. The debate about training for residential work can be pursued elsewhere, for example in Clough (1997) or the Residential Forum's (1998a and b) papers on training for residential staff. My own conclusion is that residential work is best seen as part of direct care rather than social work, and will profit from establishing its own identity.

What matters for this book is that there is consideration of the knowledge, values and skills which are necessary for work in a residential home.

For a home to function well there has to be an understanding of:

1. people: the social, medical and psychological explanations for their current state;
2. residential homes as organizations, and of the systems which can develop within them;
3. practice skills such as: *care tasks*, at mealtimes or getting up; *communication*, for example talking to people on their own, and in groups or meetings; and *searching to understand*, perhaps called assessment;
4. themselves as staff (of their own history and circumstances, and of the ways they are touched by and respond to certain events); as in other jobs where staff work with people who potentially are vulnerable, staff have to manage their feelings and not be driven by their own response to a resident's pain or disturbance.

Such understanding is needed within the establishment. But staff need skills as well as understanding, the ability to do, as well as to think. The skills are legion and include: constructing appropriate systems within the home; direct care, such as how to lift or bath someone, management in organizations; and all that goes under such deceptively easy titles as 'communication' and 'assessment'. There is no one system of staff categorization or structure: different places will work out different staffing patterns according to the nature of their work and the way in which they interpret the task.

Not everybody within a home has to be knowledgeable in all areas but everyone has to have sufficient understanding of the way in which individual tasks are a part of a larger whole and must take account of understanding of individual residents. In addition practice must have an ethical base, as developed in Chapter 6.

Understanding behaviour

At the heart of good residential practice is an attempt to understand the behaviour of residents: the reasons why people do what they do. The immense significance of theory is apparent here. Without a determined search to understand behaviour, residents will be treated in immediate response to their actions which is both inappropriate and dangerous. We have to examine the interplay between structures, cultures, environments, and individual lifestyle.

Take any of the myriad examples of behaviour: a child who does not join in with others, who attacks their work and whose performance is far below potential as indicated by test results; a younger adult with a learning disability who has refused to move out from a residential home to a house in the town; or an older adult who has just moved into a home, is eating very little, has seemed withdrawn since arrival and says that nothing is wrong. People who behave like this may be seen as 'naughty', 'awkward', 'silly' or 'ungrateful'. Searching to understand behaviour allows escape from this type of unhelpful categorization.

Deliberately I emphasize the *search* to understand because there is not one correct theory to explain the complexities of human behaviour. What theories have to offer is an insight into the background to behaviour, perhaps related to causation or motivation. Such insight allows for new interpretations of events, with the potential for different responses or treatment. In its turn a response based on an attempt to understand allows for change or healing in the individual. The best residential homes are those where the staff seek to understand: theory helps such understanding.

Theories are clusterings of ideas which attempt to explain events: in part they show up patterns which may not have been seen; in part they try to link an event with a cause. Thus, Bowlby (1969) suggested that children who have not established an early relationship with an adult (usually the mother) will find it difficult to establish trusting relationships with others. Such a theory offers an explanation of current behaviour, which in turn allows consideration of how best to work with such a child. Staff might try to provide an opportunity for the establishment of a trusting relationship with an adult: one in which the adult is reliable, with time and attention given to the child. The theory may also suggest patterns of subsequent behaviour, perhaps that although there may be some antagonistic behaviour from the child to test out whether the adult can cope, it is imperative for the adult to attempt to set clear boundaries and to hold to them.

Why theory matters

At the heart of good education is a search to understand. This demands questioning, with a refusal to be satisfied with half-truth. Students are asked to justify. Such questioning and analysis are fundamental to good residential practice. Staff should not be taking on trust from others that a style or method is either proper or inevitable: they need to be convinced that ideas make sense. Jones and Fowles (1984) contend that the theories which are adopted widely are those in which the authors have captured aspects which help people to understand their worlds; in other words, they help people make sense of what they perceive.

Theorizing allows individual questioning and searching to take place in a context or framework. People can examine what they experience and what they think against a theoretical construction. In this way debate can take place about explanation and intervention: it becomes possible to move from argument that is based on 'This is my view; trust me' to one that is reasoned. What someone perceives to be bad practice can be questioned and challenged, rather than accepted.

Without theorizing we are dependent on individual accounts and explanations: people will state a personal perspective whether on causation of behaviour or on practice.

If it is accepted, as argued here, that theorizing within a home is an essential of good practice, it is essential also to realize that theories do not provide certainties. Human behaviour is far too complex to be able to state that x happens because of y: we are in the field of probabilities. Thus theorizing plays an important part in the creation of good practice. I am not arguing that theories provide a panacea for solving all problems. Theories must inform the practice within an establishment; they must influence the climate in which each person works. Different members of staff will have different depths of knowledge: not everyone is required to be an expert theoretician.

If people strive to understand what is happening and to examine what they should do, there is the potential for practice to improve.

The development of theory for residential practice

Theorizing in residential work occurred first in work with children and young people. Primarily this took the form of individuals such as Lane, Neill, Shaw and Wills writing personal accounts of their work. In essence, these described individual children and their behaviour, together with the ways in which such behaviour was understood and managed, sometimes resulting in the children's lives being trans- formed. Implicit in such writing, occasionally explicit, is a belief that there are reasons why children behave in ways which are problematic to themselves and others, and a willingness to search for a response which did not belittle children nor further problematize their behaviour. Typically there was an unwillingness to accept given explanations of behaviour or given remedies. Individuals stressed particular aspects of treatment: for example, Lane and Wills the notion of democracy and shared responsibility; Neill and Lyward, the recognition that children do not, perhaps cannot, learn until they are ready.

Dockar-Drysdale focused more on a systematic analysis of children's behaviour, of its interpretation and thus of its management and treat- ment. She wrote less on the life of the place as a whole. Her under- standing and approach started with the individual child. She was more closely linked to mainstream child development and psychology than many other UK writers on residential work. There is an important message from this for all residential work: the starting point in under- standing children, young people and adults who live in residential homes is theory about normality; explanation of disturbance must be a part of general theory.

An example of this in practice is of students coming from experiences in residential child care to have placements in primary schools. They came to see that some behaviour which they had defined within the children's home as problematic, in reality, was normal.

The development of ideas about residential child care rather than the individuals who live in homes follows at a later stage. Beedell (1970) is the first writer in the UK to build a coherent text around understanding of children and the action that follows within the residential establishment.

In residential work with adults there has been much less writing from practitioners. So the literature has developed from outsiders analysing practice. They have written predominantly about either what it is like for adults to live in residential homes or what they consider is good practice in residential homes. There are few personal accounts by staff working with adults which tell the story of their work. What has been written has focused far more on residential work with older people than other groups of adults. There are dangers that the special characteristics of residential work with adults with learning disabilities, physical disabilities, mental illness or drug problems may get lost in attempting to adapt literature from work with older people.

It is also worth noting that in all residential work, with children as well as with adults, there has been a tendency for research to highlight what goes wrong rather than what works well. It is important to avoid a dichotomy between critical research writing and supportive practice writing.

Types of theory for residential work

Payne (1997) suggests that modern theory includes three aspects:

1. *Models* describe what happens during practice in a general way, applying to a wide range of situations, in a structured form...
2. Approaches to or *perspectives* on a complex human activity express values or views of the world which allow participants to order their minds sufficiently to be able to manage themselves while participating...
3. Explanatory '*theory*' accounts for why an action results in particular consequences and the circumstances in which it does so (p. 35).

He argues that 'most social workers use "theory" to mean ideas that influence them as opposed to things that they do in practice'(p. 37) and suggests that there are three types of social work theory: theories of what social work *is*; theories of *how to do* social work; theories of the *client world* (p. 39). My own typology of theories for residential work has some differences:

- *theories of the resident world*: such theories offer explanations as to what has been influential in residents' lives; the theories will include perspectives from sociology and psychology;
- *theories of function and task in residential care*: these examine the nature of the activity called residential work;
- *theories of intervention*: these suggest that different ways of intervening will have different results;
- *theories of residential homes as systems*: such theories examine the processes which take place within residential homes.

Theories of the resident world are those which help in understanding the lives of residents; they include propositions both as to why people behave in the ways that they do and why they are in their current position. There are three major types of explanations for people's state or condition: maturation and biological ageing, psychological development and sociological perspectives.

The first of these, *maturation and biological ageing*, considers the physical changes which happen to the body: the human body alters; in part this is growth and development as a baby changes into a physically mature human; in part this is biological ageing, in which the body begins to decline. This decline, for the most part, is gradual and not problematic for a person's lifestyle. Bond *et al.* (1993, pp. 21–2) summarize the characteristics of ageing set out by Strehler. Ageing is universal, although some people attempt to turn back the clock through cosmetic surgery or creams that it is claimed will remove wrinkles. It is also progressive, intrinsic to the organism and degenerative.

While the fact of biological ageing is universal, the process differs between people because of the impact of other factors such as environment and lifestyle. We are also hugely affected by genetics, the attributes which are passed on through heredity and include predisposition to certain diseases.

Some theories focus on a person's *psychological development*, the state of people's minds: what do people feel like? how do they perceive themselves? in what ways does psychological state influence behaviour?

For example, a psychodynamic approach proposes that a child's early experiences have an immense impact on later life. Ward (1998, pp. 11–27) outlines some of the elements of the approach. 'Winnicott would say that the capacity to sustain the sense of an inner world develops during the first year or so of life, out of the child's experience of being "held" emotionally as well as physically by the parent(s)' (p. 14). The child learns to cope with the world, to move from dependence to independence, if the quality of this holding experience has been good enough. 'The child gradually brings together (with help and holding) all of these fragmentary bits and pieces of experience to the point where he can begin to hold *himself* together – the process of ego-integration' (p. 17). Some children do not manage this integration and are not sufficiently put together: in Dockar-Drysdale's terms they are unintegrated. Children develop ways of living with unintegration but such false selves are unlikely to become integrated without help.

Ward recognizes that psychodynamic writing is rightly criticized for taking too little account of poverty and oppression, racism and gender stereotyping (p. 2) but argues that it is one valid approach to understanding and working with troubled children.

There are various theories which look at adult development. Life-span developmental psychology stresses the importance of seeing 'people in the context of their whole life history'; there are reciprocal influences between person and life-span (Bond *et al.*, 1993, p. 30). Erikson's (1950) model highlights various stages in life and outlines 'tasks' that have to be fulfilled. His ideas have influenced my understanding of being a person at different times in one's life. Thus, he suggests that in adolescence we struggle with 'ego identity (the wholeness of self) versus identity diffusion', in middle age the focus is on 'generativity', an 'interest in establishing and guiding the next generation', and in old age the tension is between ego integrity and despair. These can be seen as a combination of who we are and where we are going. Erikson does not suggest that we move on to the next task only when we have resolved the previous one; some aspects of a former task may be unresolved as we struggle with the next. Indeed, I think the tasks can be seen as ones which, whether resolved or not, stay with people throughout their lives. In middle age not only do we work at 'generativity versus stagnation': we rework earlier tasks, such as autonomy. The word 'task' may seem too specific since individuals are unlikely to see what is happening in their lives in this way. However, as a way of understanding what people have to accomplish in their lives it is helpful.

I have highlighted one particular approach which I find valuable. Bond *et al.* (1993, pp. 19–52) present a clear outline of the differences between numerous approaches to understanding old age. They cover various psychological schools and sociological perspectives, including structuralism, symbolic interactionism and labelling theory. The detail could be amended to relate to children or younger adults and stands out as a clear description of different types of explanation.

The third major type of explanation is that of *sociological perspectives*. All sociological perspectives have in common a focus on the ordered nature of society – that is, a belief that in most situations the range of possible actions is fairly limited and we have a fair idea of how we would behave as well as being able to predict, within limits, the behaviour of others (Bond *et al.*, 1993, p. 31).

There are different frameworks of sociological explanation. Structuralists assert that the structures of society determine people's lives: people are defined and limited by the social constructions of class, gender, ethnicity, disability, age, family and work status. Other sociologists examine the meaning that people attach to things and events. A third school would look at the way in which people are exploited by processes of industrialization. These include the division between capital and labour, and the processes that exist in our current society, which some term 'post-industrialization'. Any of these sociological explanations state that people's identities are constructed by such processes, and that people live their lives in the context of such construction. These influence, some would say determine, how others (and indeed we ourselves) perceive us.

It is sometimes presumed that biological and psychological ageing go hand in hand. This is incorrect: people may age biologically in that they become less able to manage certain physical tasks but continue at the same level in terms of learning or management of situations. Indeed, in some respects people may develop new skills.

Theories may be mutually exclusive; alternatively, they may provide partial explanation. Thus people's health is influenced by environment and by lifestyle. I am using the term 'environment' to cover a number of factors external to the individual. These would include the physical environment as it affects individuals: the quality of air and water, housing, transport and local facilities. The environment in which we live will have a massive impact on our lives. In the UK, poverty is perhaps the single factor that best explains variations in people's health. Having poor housing or being isolated from shops and leisure facilities dramatically affects daily living and may influence someone's move to a residential home.

By contrast 'lifestyle' is used in different ways. At times it is a term that does no more than describe differences in how people live. I am using the word to recognize that whatever major level of explanation is adopted, people have choices, however small, as to how they will live. Thus, in this sense, lifestyle describes a person's response to their circumstances. To take a simple example, whether people take more or less exercise will influence their health. Adults may get more exercise in looking after their own home than they may in a residential home. The extent to which people have scope to control aspects of their lives is subject to debate.

I have already noted that psychodynamic theory has been criticized on the grounds that it has been developed in white, North European and North American cultures and takes little account of the ways in which people's lives are determined by structural forces. The criticism is valid in terms of the theory as it was originally postulated. However, theory does not have to be static; it can be challenged and amended. So it is legitimate to consider whether there are aspects of any theory that can be reinterpreted in the light of current understanding.

Some theories endeavour to examine what it is that makes people do well. Insofar as these look at psychological success as well as material success, most work has been done on 'successful ageing'. In this field a debate has taken place, predominantly between advocates of *disengagement* and *activity* theories. In brief, Cumming and Henry (1961) suggested that people aged successfully if they and society were involved in a mutual process of withdrawal from former roles. Havighurst (1963) countered that those who aged successfully were people who replaced work activity with other work-like tasks. By and large the activity theorists have held sway. Coleman (1993, p. 84) points out that the original disengagement theory was a reaction against the idea that ageing was 'intrinsically deteriorative': Cumming and Henry argued that there was a more positive role for older people in society and, significantly, that people were given a degree of licence 'to express themselves freely'.

The discussion today has moved beyond the 'either disengagement or activity' argument, to what best allows people to control their lives and to maintain self-worth. Parallel points could be considered in relation to younger adults. It should also be noted that in this field theories have been developed largely in relation to the dominant white community: we know little of how first- and second-generation migrants age success-fully, nor of differences between cultures in perspectives on successful ageing. If for some there is a focus in old age on identity and meaning of life, how is identity to be understood in different ethnic groups? Indeed, what is the place of ethnic identity? In the UK Blakemore has done most to bring ethnicity to the fore in discussions of both ageing and service provision. (See, in particular, Blakemore, 1989, 1993; Blakemore and Boneham, 1993; Fenton, 1986; Ford and Sinclair's, 1987, account of Asian women's description of ageing.)

Theories of function and task in residential care examine the nature of the activity which is called 'residential work'. How does it mesh with welfare policies? What link is there between task in residential care and the wider debates for example about dependency or the nature of community? At another level, is residential care a branch of social work or a discrete category in its own right? Is residential care better seen as a type of direct care, which might be practised in other settings such as people's own homes or day-care centres? Alternatively, is the notion of generic residential work unhelpful to work in specific settings? The last question leads to consideration of residential work as a category of differently structured disciplines perhaps seeing the core expertise as children, physical disability, mental illness, learning disability or old age.

Whatever grouping is adopted it is helpful to think about the primary task, that is the task for which the organization exists. For example, Beedell (1970) looked at the components of bringing up children in society to analyse task and practice in residential homes for children and young people. He describes a consequent function of residential care as *parenting*. He stresses that he does not mean that residential units should try to be parents to the children: he is attempting to describe the core task within a residential home. The function of parenting involves three aspects: holding, nurturing and the development of ego integrity. This type of theorizing about residential practice is immensely important for it allows consideration of the nature of the activity.

It is perhaps in this area of function that some of the greatest uncertainties and confusions about residential work have arisen. Thus there are arguments that residential homes have in part contained groups of people away from their own homes and communities because in society as a whole, people preferred not to be confronted with the disability or the problems of residents. This proposition is sometimes interpreted as an attack on residential establishments: rather, it is a sharp review of society's attitudes towards individual people.

However, analysis of function does allow a study of the performance of residential homes: what are the results of living in a residential home? The evidence on this will be reviewed later but here it is important to note that some commentators have argued for the scrapping of residential homes. Indeed, students on some social work training courses have felt that the critique has undermined practice.

I have described 'the basic task that is common to all residential homes' as the creation of:

> a base for living and, within that, to carry out the tasks of daily living in the best possible way. Anything else that is needed, for example counselling, is secondary to this and indeed cannot be carried out effectively if the arrangements for daily living are not carefully planned. (Clough, 1982, p. 47)

Miller and Gwynne recognized that most of the residents in their 1972 study of homes for people with physical disabilities would spend the rest of their lives in the home. They produce three different models of residential care. In the *warehousing model*, residents are treated as bodies to be processed, the equivalent of raw materials in a factory; they start dirty and emerge clean. By contrast, the *horticultural model* is one in which the person's potential is recognized, the focus is on development. Yet this model fails to recognize that people may not be able, or want, to develop new skills. Miller and Gwynne argue for an *organizational* model which will 'provide... the opportunities [for residents] to follow the route' they choose, with staff supporting them in implementing their decision. Consequently they propose a model with three components: *organization for dependence*; *organization for independence*; and *organization for support* (pp. 161, 188–208).

Theorizing about practice is the next category, *theories of intervention*: these suggest that different ways of intervening will have varying results. In this category would be psychodynamic or behavioural strategies, or interventions in systems. Such theories are drawn from disciplines outside residential care, though theorists about residential care may have contributed to the development of the theories, perhaps most notably with psychodynamic approaches to residential work with children and young people. Dockar-Drysdale, Wills and Lyward are just a few among many others. Included also in this section would be theories about communicating with people or working in groups, again drawn from wider practice theory and adapted to residential work.

With Allan Brown I have written about the nature of groups in residential and day care, what we term 'the mosaic of groups and groupings'. It is imperative to ensure that theories from other disciplines are examined for their appropriateness to residential work. Nevertheless, there are distinctive characteristics to being in a group in a residential home.

Most theories on groups refer to small, formal groups which meet on regular occasions but for limited amounts of time. Life in a residential home is markedly different. People move in and out of groupings throughout a day. People may be in set groups for some events, but are likely to have frequent contact outside that group event with the staff and residents. Group work writing hardly acknowledges this and there are few models for a type of grouping which is neither like a family nor a formal group (Brown and Clough, 1989). Indeed, the term 'group care', which has been applied by some to all residential life, fails to recognize how much time people spend in interactions between individuals: resident with resident; and resident with staff member.

In the same way, drawing on theories of communication and interviewing can be unhelpful if it fails to recognize that most communication in a residential home does not take place in formal interviews. Typically conversation between staff and residents occurs during other events: meals, bathing or washing up.

> Conversations would pass from table to table, from person to person, like a ball game... But talking went on everywhere... [Conversations] were important, because they helped to allow new and changed attitudes to take shape. (Pick, 1981, p. 82)

In terms of intervention in systems, it is argued that it may be possible to intervene in different places to achieve a desired end result. Thus, to help a resident who has difficulty in communicating who is teased by others, it would be possible to influence various parts of the system: the *individual* resident could be helped to develop skills or self-confidence; or there could be attempts to influence the person's circle of friends, the wider resident group, staff group or the culture of the establishment as a whole, whether by calling a community meeting or introducing an anti-harassment policy. Some of these could be tried simultaneously. The point being stressed is the idea known as *equifinality*, that it is possible to bring about the same outcome through action in different parts of a system.

The fourth category of theories is that of *residential homes as systems*. These examine the ways in which what happens within a residential home can be seen as part of a system. For example, I have reworked the theories of institutionalization of Goffman and others to highlight their relevance to today's much smaller residential homes. I suggested that, rather than inevitable processes, there are *institutional tendencies*: these are processes which can be countered but have the potential to dominate life in a residential home. Thus there are tendencies or pressures:

for people to lose or to be stripped of their identity when they move in;

for residents to feel powerless;

for a person's privacy to be invaded;

for residents and workers to seem to be on opposite sides, as 'us' and 'them';

for it to be easier to care for people in groups than separately...

for (some workers) to find the task beyond them and end up controlling residents in ways which they would have found unacceptable when they started. (Clough, 1993: pp. 79–80)

Further, the consideration of the *residential home as system* allows study of the way the structures and organization of the home influence practice. This has been recognized for a long time. In an extract quoted in Chapter 2, Menzies (1959) contends that children will behave with more responsibility towards food if the staff who have immediate responsibility for their care are given greater responsibility for its organization. Again, as mentioned earlier, King *et al.* (1971) state that in the units they studied the quality of the daily care of children was higher in those places where staff had more control of their boundaries, for example in employment of staff, organizing staffing rotas, or ordering food and other goods. Theories of organizations and of management make an important contribution in this category.

It would be useful also to consider the interaction of the residential home with the external systems that impinge on it.

Theory in work with people

The theory that is used in residential work derives from different disciplines: *psychology* (stages of development, explanations for 'normal' and 'abnormal' behaviour); *sociology* (the effects of environment and structures on people, poverty, gender, ethnicity, socio-economic grouping); *philosophy* (moral values, religion and spirituality) and *social psychology* (the relationship of the individual to the world).

These subjects should be common for many professions in which staff work with people. In addition to the general knowledge about people and environment from the topics above, staff need knowledge specific to the activity in which they are engaged, whether that be teaching, nursing or residential work. This knowledge of task in residential work (holding, nurture and development) and of process has to be related to a number of factors: people and their characteristics; methods, outcomes and worker style.

A conversation between worker and individual must be seen in the context of this knowledge. The worker may hold a light-hearted conversation with an individual but, when working well, will do so with knowledge of that person. At other times the conversation will be far more focused and deliberate: perhaps to try to help one person attempt something which has defeated them on other occasions, to face another with aspects of behaviour or to try to understand a third person's seeming depression.

Theory may seem to outsiders or to staff within a home either as a luxury or an irrelevance: what matters, the argument would run, is being able to get on with the job now. I remember hearing of the head of a large approved school who said that what he wanted was staff who could get the boys up in the morning and down to breakfast on time. The implication was that it was practical not theoretical skills that were needed. The point is valid: theory that leads to an inability to manage one's work is of no use. My contention is that the way the job is undertaken must be informed by theory. It is common for students on social work training courses to want to get on with what they regard as the real work, the work with people, and to find difficulty in describing how they use theory in practice. In this sense theory may seem to be an artificial constraint that requires workers to fit their activities into boxes that do not match the way they practise.

However, 'the getting on with the job' should be influenced by this process of theorizing and reflection. Practice must be informed by knowledge, not consequent solely on the views, skills, experiences and attitudes of individual staff. What is wanted also is knowledge that is accessible and explainable to all staff and indeed to residents and others.

Take the example of a young adult with a learning disability who has been quiet for several meals and suddenly is embroiled in a number of quarrels with other residents. The response of staff should be informed by their understanding of this person, of others, of the style of the home and of the current atmosphere. This does not mean that there will be space for the staff member to spend a lengthy period in reflection: it does mean that the staff member's way of analysing what is happening and of deciding what to do should be embedded in theory.

Subsequently, staff should be able to review explanations for events and review options. They need to be able to account for their actions. Without such capacity a charismatic or powerful personality may go unchallenged.

Theorizing leads to a presentation of ideas and thus confronts people with questions that at other times they may choose to avoid. Different explanations show variations in whether problems are seen to be individual or collective: 'You have problems in controlling yourself' is one perspective; another is, 'Society is creating the conditions in which there is no role for people like you to lead a fulfilled life.' Thus, theories contribute to the debate as to the extent to which people can or should be held responsible for their current state. For example, if we consider the reasons for a person's behaviour, some theories will stress biochemical influences on the body, others the way in which behaviour is learnt as a consequence of systems in which people have lived. Some theories will be seen as determinist in that they present reasons for behaviour which lie outside the control of the individual. Others will emphasize the control or responsibility of individuals.

Intervention or practice theories propose ideas for action. They have to be judged in relation both to their effectiveness and to their morality. The existence of theories should not lead to a mechanistic adoption of a particular approach.

Some years ago I visited a residential home for adults which used group reinforcement to control drug dependence. There were clear expectations of how individuals should use their time in the establishment, including talking about themselves in the group and taking responsibility for self and others. Some people who failed in these expectations had to wear placards round their necks of the type 'I cannot control my temper'. I dislike this sort of humiliation but the management argued that this was the most effective way to change addictive behaviour *and* that the individuals had come to the place knowing that this was the approach that would be adopted. I am not trying to propose an answer to this: I am highlighting the importance of taking moral decisions as to practice.

Theories may be offered as single explanations or as part explanations to be taken in conjunction with other theories.

One of the difficulties in analysis is that of determining whether the behaviour is the consequence of what happens within the residential home, of what has happened before someone moves in or of factors external to the home. There are significant consequences for understanding residential work. Thus some loose generalization on institutions has held residential staff or residential systems responsible for far more of the residents' behaviour than is reasonable. It is forgotten, for example, that some of the young people in residential homes are those who have been expelled both from school and their homes: some are people whom nobody seems able to manage; some leave a residential home to return to chaotic situations.

The reverse can also happen: places which create good systems for managing children, perhaps with firm boundaries together with a child-centred approach to understanding their problems, may find that children behave well for periods within the home. Rather than being praised for their success, it may be assumed that the children were never as difficult as had been presumed.

The purpose of theorizing is to promote thinking so that practice is improved. Beedell (1970, p. 19) writes about one of the aspects of parenting, holding:

> All societies have customs and rituals designed to ensure the dependent child's survival and to protect him from danger, discomfort and distress. In doing so they give the child mainly good experiences of care, comfort and control. In the residential context we can call this the *holding* aspect of provision.

From this we can consider the characteristics of the young people at a particular home: what sort of holding do they want and need? what will be the complexities of holding these residents? This has to be followed with theorizing about practice: how are we to hold these residents? what does it mean in terms of day-to-day practice? do different approaches have different results? and so on.

Misuse of theory

Here must be noted a further proviso on the use of theories. There is a tendency to take them to be universal truths which apply to all people living through such events. This is rarely the case: what theories offer are explanations which need to be tested against individual circumstances. A theory is an explanation for events; it is not 'truth'.

Ian McEwan has a character, Stephen, in his novel *The Child in Time* (1987). Stephen finds himself debating the age at which children should learn to read.

It was that old business of theorizing, taking up a position, planting the flag of identity and self-esteem, then fighting all comers to the end.

And there was no richer field for speculation assertively dressed as fact than child care... For three centuries, generations of experts, priests, moralists, social scientists, doctors – mostly men – had been pouring out instructions and ever-mutating facts for the benefit of mothers.

He had read the solemn pronouncements on... how children should be allowed to do whatever they want so that their divine natures can blossom, and how it is never too soon to break a child's will. (p. 80)

Theories used like a blunderbuss are harmful rather than helpful: I have known examples where staff presume that they know what is in the best interests of a resident from a superficial drawing on theory. Thus, staff might move from recognizing that *frequently* people at times of crisis follow certain stages, and that they must be allowed to do so if they are to deal positively with their experiences, to presuming that all people *must* go through certain stages for their future benefit. This may result in forcing a period of grieving on residents.

The potential harm is apparent. Theories are general explanations: they are not inevitabilities. Some people may not grieve for their past or may choose to manage their present by 'putting a brave face' on events. Staff would exercise their power inappropriately if they refused to allow residents to work out how they wanted to manage events. At an extreme, the presumption based on theoretical inevitability results in a view that everybody goes through certain processes and must be encouraged to do so 'for their own good'. We must remind ourselves how dangerous are the words 'for their own good', the assumptions that lie behind them and the consequences that flow from them.

Theory in residential work should not be used to exclude others: it is possible to express complex ideas in understandable language. In this respect residential work is like social work: it must draw on a theoretical base, but it must share that theory with others. Too often staff may describe the theory in language that others cannot understand, either because they do not properly understand it themselves or because they wish to enhance their own status.

On the other hand, nobody should be attempting to put into effect ideas that are not properly understood. At times people want to claim an understanding that they do not have, whether to fit in with the practice in a home or to enhance their standing as 'experts'.

Equally worrying is that there have been occasions when people did not think that what was being said made sense but kept quiet because of the claimed expertise of another. In one enquiry into child abuse practices it emerged that several people had doubted the methods but had been silenced by the claims to expertise of the head of the unit (Levy and Kahan, 1991).

The same enquiry also showed the way in which theories can be improperly understood or distorted. The head of the home claimed to be a follower of Dockar-Drysdale and to be using regression as a tool. In reality, instead of a child-centred approach (searching for an understanding of current behaviour from past experiences, and using this to help work out how best to help the child), the head adopted a style of forcing his interpretation on children and demanding that they regress, in the sense of behaving like younger children. So there is a change from theoretical approaches in which children who have missed out on important early experiences are allowed the opportunity to experience these, to a rigid and authoritarian imposition on children.

Conclusion

Nevertheless, good theorizing adds a depth to residential practice. It is as staff and residents strive to understand what is happening within the home that not only the most creative but the most resident-centred work takes place. The willingness to search and the struggle to understand are characteristics that people recognize in others around them.

5

Using Knowledge in Practice: Getting on with the Job

Having examined in the last two chapters some of what is known about residential work, I focus in this chapter on the use of such information in practice.

Residents' experiences

It is obvious that a move into a residential home, the experience of 'becoming a resident', is a major life change. How can we understand what it is like?

We can get some clues from what people themselves say. So, in a study of a home for older people 20 years ago, residents said:

I have been in a good many places. I soon fell in.

I was excited about coming in. Surprised to see such a wonderful place.

I felt pleased with the way I was greeted.

The most important thing was feeling comfortable – nothing to worry about; able to rest; done my duty; surprised at such a place.

I think a lot about what I left behind – little treasures… I miss the life around my home.

I was used to institutions. The cooking is all right but it's not like home. I miss the salt though…

I miss the phone, my own possessions… the friends, the control of the TV.

I miss not having enough to do, but got used to it. (Clough, 1981, pp. 75–6)

Knowledge into practice

There is now considerable evidence of the characteristics of good practice from the perspectives of different stakeholders. In other words, we
know a lot about the components of good residential practice in any
setting: first, there has to be a clear statement of the purpose of the
home; second, the values and objectives should be agreed as widely as
possible; and, third, the style should be resident centred.

Thus, one registration authority states that all homes '*must* produce
clear statements which outline their policy, and these should be sufficiently detailed for residents and others to know the sort of home into
which they are considering moving' (Cumbria Social Services Inspectorate). The second factor requires that there is agreement on values, in
particular between staff and residents and among the staff team, but
also more widely with relatives, external managers, other professionals
and the community. This is developed in Chapter 6. Here I shall focus
on the third characteristic, a *resident-centred approach*.

Parker (1988) notes the information from various studies that
different regimes have differential effects on children's behaviour: the
best results are achieved by child-orientated rather than institution-
orientated practices.

> [In]... retrospective accounts provided by adults and young people who had been
> in care it is the sense of receiving understanding, sympathetic, comforting and
> individual attention which stands out as the hallmark of the experiences which
> they cherish. (p. 111)

> Establishments do 'best' when the children feel they are cared for, listened to and
> responded to in a quiet, sympathetic, and consistent fashion. (p. 115)

The term 'resident-centred', my term for what Parker describes as
'child-orientated', easily trips off the tongue. I shall pursue the characteristics of resident-centred practice.

● *The starting point is an attempt to* understand the resident: this is an
   active search, a pursuit of understanding, premised on the belief that
   there are reasons for behaviour and that understanding them will help
   in caring for the resident; such understanding should draw on
   theoretical frameworks that account for a person's behaviour; theories
   should be related to the particular circumstances of a particular
   resident; to this should be added the perspective of residents on their
   experiences before moving to the home and since arrival.

- *The daily life within the home is built from an attempt to* produce systems that best match residents' wants and needs.

- *There is time within the daily routine to* listen to individual residents.

- *Residents are involved in* negotiations about life in the establishment.

- *Staff worry about residents*: they are concerned for residents, hold on to their interests and continue to think about what will work best for them, even when they are not with residents.

- *Residents must feel that they are at the centre of life in the home*, that their interests and well-being matter to staff. There is a pressure within any group for the system maintenance to drive lifestyle. This can be seen in families where rigid systems may be established which somehow forget or displace individuals. Within residential homes the process is more powerful and known as institutionalization: completing the task becomes more important than the reason why the task is being undertaken. Thus, at times residents in homes for adults have been got up very early in the morning and helped to bed very early at night to suit staffing arrangements or someone's ideas of what might be termed 'neatness' in practice.

I include 'worry about' and 'being concerned for' in the description to try to capture the element of staff interest and involvement in the lives of residents. Triseliotis and Russell (1984) compared the outcomes of children who were adopted with those from residential care. One of their findings is that the health of adopted children was better than children from residential homes.

When I first read this book, I was surprised by this finding as I would have expected that residential homes in the period being studied would have had good checks for teeth and general health. There are many possible explanations ranging from differences in diet to the possibility that the adopted children were happier and that this affected their health. However, I suspect the explanation may lie more in the way in which in families people show their concern for others by noticing changes in their appearance and their behaviour. Family members may be persistent in suggesting that the person should see the doctor or do something about the matter. Of course, in close relationships such concern can turn into bullying and the same is true for residential care. Nevertheless, the concern for the well-being of another is essential. The key to good experience for the residents is that they feel they matter, that they are cared for and cared about.

In effect, the experience of the resident should be at the heart of practice. External management, internal management and staff all have to recognize that the establishment must be founded on this essential. Whatever is said by staff and others, residents will know from their experiences whether decisions are made and systems developed that are consequent on their wants and needs. External management, often under pressure, has to protect the boundaries of the home so that it is able to function in this way. This is not the same as arguing, improperly and impossibly, that whatever a resident wants is to be done. It is stating that the primary task of the place must be built around the resident and that the primary task must be maintained if residents are to have good experiences.

The ways residents experience living in a residential home is not always understood by others. There are a lot of reasons why staff and others may not understand the nature of the experience:

- the staff may not see it as important to understand residents;
- they may be very busy, finding difficulty in getting through the tasks they have to accomplish;
- their perception of residents' experience, sharp when they started as residential workers, may have become blunted;
- awareness may be disturbing; they cannot face the reality of others' pain;
- staff may think that they can understand the experience, using words like empathy, but may miss aspects related to individuals or groups; this is particularly significant in relation to the assumptions that are made about others in relation to gender, ethnicity, sexual orientation, culture, class, disability and age.

Staff assumptions influence practice. Whitaker *et al.* (1984) found that staff were likely to think that children should be left to sort out their problems themselves; in the process of children sorting out their problems, many young people were bullied.

> Thirty out of the thirty four children (from different homes) reported personally experienced physical abuse, verbal tormenting, feelings of intense aggravation with other children, and/or alarm at witnessing aggressive exchanges between other children... Those who bullied others tended to see themselves as having been provoked by their victims. Children who bullied others were often bullied themselves on other occasions. (p. 15)

This is a sharp reminder that the intent of staff, perhaps to establish environments in which young people will be a positive resource for others, is not necessarily achieved.

Of course, in many residential homes staff do manage to create a style in which the community is managed in a way that is purposeful and in which residents are supportive of others. My point is that an intent to do this does not mean necessarily that it will happen. Research can be helpful in showing the reality of residential living.

I conclude this section with a list of pointers from different writers of components of good practice. Kahan (1994) examines the key pointers to providing good and consistent care for the difficult child:

> Care and assessment as repeating and linked activities.
>
> To the extent that a child will allow, work needs to be done on the problems which led to admission to the home or school.
>
> Consistency does not mean the same for everyone.
>
> Do not gloss over the evident concerns in the hope that they will go away when the child has settled in.
>
> Keep other professionals right up to date and require their support, advice and direct intervention.
>
> Residential child care is teamwork within a competent workplace. (pp. 111–15)

Gibbons (1988, pp. 190ff.), in reviewing establishments for people who are mentally ill, claims, as many others, that smaller regimes which are self-contained are more successful than larger wards. In using such points it is essential to know what it is that these character-istics are designed to achieve; some larger homes, structured in partic-ular ways, may be successful.

In his review of residential child care, Parker (1988) states that the evidence on the effects of different regimes shows that establishments do best when:

> children feel they are cared for, listened to and responded to in a quiet, sympa-thetic and consistent fashion;
>
> atmosphere and quality are linked to leadership which is influenced by training;
>
> for a home to have enduring influence there is need for 'a reasonable agreement' from all parties as to goals and how to achieve them; account has to be taken of external social and economic forces;
>
> children are best settled and have most chance of returning home when contact with parents is actively maintained;

privacy is essential;

children feel stigmatized and steps can be taken to minimize that hurt;

and with adolescents in particular:

establishments do well when young people see themselves as acquiring instrumental skills;

it is important to start to equip with the social skills for independent living as early as possible;

clear, consistent and firm control is necessary. (p. 115, in part summarized)

Thus, there is considerable knowledge of the factors which are conducive to successful practice. What is much less clear is how to create the environment which will allow these factors to develop. In other words, how is 'clear, consistent and firm control' to be produced? In particular, how is this to happen when circumstances are not favourable, perhaps the young people are antagonistic to staff, the local community is intolerant of the home and the staff themselves have lost confidence?

Moving in to a residential home

In the previous chapter I showed that there are disputes as to the reasons why people are in their current physical and psychological state. I shall move on to consider how theories can influence our understanding of 'a journey to residence' and how to use such knowledge in practice.

Becoming a resident is a consequence of a person's current life state. While we cannot state that becoming a resident is caused by any one factor, we can show the sorts of factors which make residence more likely. We have to content ourselves with knowing that there is an interaction between societal structures and psychological state. Parents may find it difficult to cope with children because of their poverty, low opinion of themselves and poor housing. Others may presume things about them or their children because of attributes such as class, ethnicity, gender or sexual orientation. The response to children causing repeated disturbance at school will vary with how they are perceived. People are placed in categories and labelled. Young people in residential homes have an above average likelihood to:

- come from lower socio-economic groups;
- be regarded as troublesome rather than troubled; the description of behaviour becomes a label which influences the route of the journey; in part this will affect whether someone goes to a special school rather than a residential home;
- be from households which are unstable in the sense that members change frequently both before and during their stay in the home;
- be male.

Adults who move into residential homes come from all socio-economic groups. There are far more women than men, accounted for by the fact that women live longer than men and are less likely to have a partner alive to help with their care. Certain minority ethnic groups are *underrepresented*, in particular people of Pakistani and Indian background. The fact that there are clusters of people from minority ethnic groups in certain localities highlights local problems and the problems for those residents where there is nobody else in the home from their culture. There are still examples of residents of homes unable to speak English and having nobody with whom to talk.

In contrast with young people, adults are more likely to be regarded as 'unable to cope', than troublesome. Relatives in particular, but also GPs, may think they will be safer in a home or be less trouble. Prospective adult residents may see themselves in one of two groups: either they had made the decision themselves, even perhaps against advice or wishes of family or they see family members as having determined their future, and probably having rejected them (Clough, 1981, pp. 64–7).

We know also that people are influenced by their life experiences, in particular those in their families and close relationships. Whether or not family members want an older person to live with them seems to depend far more on the interpretation people have of their family experiences than on class. Patterns of usage of residential homes for adults do vary with culture. For example, it is noted that there are comparatively few older residents of Asian origin. This is consequent on the failure of residential homes to provide what is wanted as well as a continuing notion of family responsibility, at least with first-generation immigrants.

Some years ago it was presumed that the older people who became residents of homes had particular personality types: they were less assertive, more prone to depression. Work by Tobin and Lieberman (1976) in America challenged this idea. They found that factors other than personality types must be used to account for who does and who does not move into a home. Moves to homes were better explained by 'accumulated losses', the experience of a number of losses to self in terms of health and of other people. Theories can challenge taken-for-granted ideas.

Many people will regard a move to a home as an indication of failure, of themselves, their environment or their families. Nevertheless, we must not lose sight of the fact that for some people a move to a home is regarded as a special opportunity, perhaps for treatment, care or development of new skills.

Thus we know factors which are predictive of a greater likelihood of moving into a home. However, each person's move to a home will also be consequent on individual circumstances. It is easy to see that there are links between socio-economic group, work status, housing and environment. Any of these will have an impact on a person's capacity to continue to live in their existing circumstances.

What, then, are the factors which influence moves of older people into residential homes? Comparatively few older people themselves initiate a move into a home. Indeed, the attitude of family members towards moves to residential homes is a major influence in whether the person will make such a move. Events such as a spell in hospital often precede a move, breaking established patterns and allowing people to review their circumstances. Professionals see two major reasons for a move to a residential home: inability of the person to cope and an inadequate support system. Once a decision has been made, a move to a home tends to be rapid, with little time for planning and adjustment (Clough, 1981, pp. 63–79). By contrast, younger adults are more likely to be involved in decisions about residential care than either their younger or older counterparts.

This knowledge is relevant to staff in two ways. It should lead to an awareness of the impact of moving on residents and therefore to trying to include a prospective resident in planning.

Impact of moving to residential homes. Understanding the relationship between people and their world helps to free staff from holding residents responsible for living in a home. If staff are to be able to plan for residents moving into a home, then they must be aware of the significance of the event for residents. Thirty years ago Stevenson (1968) entitled a paper 'Reception into care – its meaning for all concerned' to capture this:

there is a need to try and get inside the meaning of this experience to him. Kindness and warmth are not enough. There must be awareness of those details of a child's behaviour and speech which may give us the clue as to how he is feeling. (p. 10)

Noting the suffering that is likely to precede a move into a home, she writes:

All this makes the theme of reception into care sound sad, even depressing. But only by recognizing the truth about this infinitely complicated process can we begin to lay the foundations for good work... we need to look for the truth and depth of this experience for everyone involved in it. This demands courage and honesty from the professional workers. But it also offers a constructive and positive approach to an action which might otherwise seem destructive and negative. (p. 17)

For residents the move is to a new life-stage. Residents manage the change in different ways: some maintain a picture of their part in decision making and consider the move to be welcome; others, with perceptions of decisions made for and about them, will feel defeated.

The experience of moving into a home is often seen as one of loss: perhaps loss of people, loss of home, loss of ability, loss of former lifestyle and loss of status. Coleman (1993, p. 98) noting that 'loss is a common element in many old people's lives', comments that the resilience of older people is neglected. Change, he suggests, occurs in many stages of adult life: 'if old age has a special character in this regard it is the likelihood of *unwanted* changes occurring'.

Understanding the experience of loss for residents is valuable. The work of Kubler-Ross (1969) and Parkes (1986) on death and bereavement has been generalized to propose patterns of loss. Kubler-Ross set out reactions to impending death; denial; anger; bargaining; depression; and acceptance. Thus staff, working with an understanding that residents may deny the full impact of their loss at moving, appropriately would ensure that they did not try to jolly the resident out of any unhappiness along the lines of: 'You don't want to look back: look forward to all the good things that you can do here; you've got no worries any more.' They would recognize the importance of residents having space to reflect on their loss.

Such analysis is helpful but must be used with caution. In relation to death, these stages may not be applicable to all cultures and certainly are not for all people. Professionals who presume that people must grieve in a particular way end up imposing their theoretical stance on others. This is even more the case when the specific theory on death is translated into other areas of loss. The insight that people *may* respond to other losses in similar ways as to death and bereavement is helpful provided that we escape from the view that theories are inevitabilities.

Mrs Carpenter, in Susan Hill's (1989) novel *A Change for the Better*, lives in a hotel with her husband after his retirement. When he dies Mrs Carpenter's response shocks others:

'I will not give way to old age and death', she said in a firm voice. 'I will not go into a decline and live off the kindness of others because I am now a widow. No I have quite decided to take myself in hand at once'. (p. 188)

Neighbours are appalled that she looks so well and happy. But they do not know of what goes on in private, of the long nights when she lay awake in her room.

'He was alone', she said to herself a hundred times a day, 'he was alone, there was nobody to help. He was alone'. At night Mrs Flora Carpenter wept, but she said nothing about any of it aloud, nothing to anyone. (p. 190)

Another way to think about a move to a home is to think about the event as a crisis. Caplan (1964) has written on intervention in crisis, arguing that if people can be helped to cope during the crisis, their functioning may return to former levels or even improve. The danger in the crisis is that people give up and manage their lives less well than before the event. The relevance for residential work is that active support for people at the time of a move may make a long-term difference to their lifestyle. Marshall (1983, p. 39) states: 'the crisis is the state of personal distress'; it has to be defined by the sufferer; people are vulnerable at times of crisis and may take decisions they will regret; practical help is important, as is the support of staying calm.

The search to understand the experience of the resident remains the key to good practice, and requires that assumptions and theory are re-evaluated and adapted. For example, Robertson (1958) studied young children in hospitals and residential nurseries: the findings showed that on the departure of their parents children went through stages of response leading in the end to withdrawal and apathy. There had been a tendency for nurses to view this withdrawn stage as 'acceptance' or 'being settled' – after all the children had changed from being angry and upset to being far less overtly disturbed. Robertson argued that it was difficult for children to recover from this apathy and despair. His view was that parents should stay in touch with their children even though this led to repeated upset for the children and that children should build attachments to individual members of staff.

A move into a residential home encourages recall of other experiences of moving house and, for many people, of the satisfaction or dissatisfaction with their current life. Earlier references to Erikson (1950) and life-span developmental psychology remind us that people faced by such transitions may reflect on the significance of their lives: what sort of person am I? what do others think of me? what have I made of my life? will I be able to do the things I want?

Erikson's mid-life task of generativity raises questions for younger adults in homes as to the focus of their lives. Given that, in our society, there is so much emphasis on work as the way in which we demonstrate our capacity to ourselves and others, those unable to get jobs are likely to wonder what they want to do with their lives and what is their standing with other people. Given also the glorification of independence and the dismissal of dependency, the questioning is likely to be particularly sharp for those who need the support of staff for daily living tasks.

There is no certainty as to what comprises identity. Residents arrive with their past, their history; they also arrive with their present: gender, ethnicity, culture, socio-economic group, sexual orientation.

Planning for a move should follow from an attempt to understand the experience of the journey to residence. Residents are likely to adjust their perceptions of self *before* they move into a residential home, seeing themselves as someone with a changed social role. This makes critical the period before the move. The staff of the residential home can help prospective residents to rehearse the move to come by providing information on lifestyle or holding discussions about arrangements for visitors. The future residents may want to visit, perhaps to remind themselves of the building and the environment, to meet residents and staff or to get more of a feel of what life will be like. In the period before someone moves in, the resident can begin to rework the expectation of the move, especially to think about the potential at times of change to do things differently.

Discussions about the prospective resident's former life are also important so that the person comes with a history, and can think about what is important to them in terms of pattern of the day and how they want to live. It is easy for people to slot into what they think is expected of them – and this has to be countered before a move.

Some residential homes require a positive statement from prospective residents that they want to move there. Others will involve the incoming resident in planning:

- the furniture and possessions to be brought in;
- the changes and adaptations to the room (mobility aids; special bed; carpets to be changed; decoration; furniture moved; pictures to be hung);
- the installation of equipment, for example a phone or computer.

This is an area of practice where knowledge of what is important to residents may not be enough. Residents may need help to think about what they want to do but then may need active assistance to make the changes they plan, perhaps to adapt a room for their use.

There are also decisions as to the timing of the move: what suits the resident? what suits the home?

Experiencing the move. Mr Jepson described what he felt about moving:

> I miss my independence. I didn't like it for three months till I got into the rhythm. Very handy, rather like it now – terrific things to get used to. I was used to deciding things for myself – cleaning, sewing when I wanted. I'd been in the army, used to discipline – the feeding arrangements didn't upset me. Living with other people is difficult, I can't describe it. (Clough, 1981, p. 76)

Such knowledge may help staff to understand that residents have to manage complex feelings. It is natural for staff, consciously or unconsciously, to look for gratitude from residents for all the hard work they put into trying to make the change a positive one. However, residents may be withdrawn (and appear ungrateful) not because the staff effort is inappropriate or because they are miserable people; it may be that they are caught up in reviewing and perhaps mourning their past. It is likely that they will find the adaptation strange.

There is evidence that people develop patterns of behaviour in response to what they perceive to be expectations of those around them. Informal processes, perhaps the culture of the resident group, may set long-term patterns for the incoming resident. People learn what is expected of them, and are particularly vulnerable to adopt what others expect when they are uncertain in a new setting. The task for staff is to find ways:

- to welcome people;
- to negotiate with residents as to what immediate arrangements they want: do they want help with unpacking? what do they want to do about medication, arrangements with visitors, meeting other residents?

- to work with residents to construct the way they want to live: finding out what they expect to find difficult, and what is important to them; developing the sort of practical help which they want in the home.

Other aspects of theory are also helpful. There is evidence that at times of residents' moves, links with other people can get broken: the resident may not have the energy to put into maintaining the link; others in their network, feeling guilty or relieved at the move, may fail to keep contact. Thus staff may need to be thoughtful as to how to welcome visitors and to assist residents in maintaining links. I remember a student on placement thinking about a welcome pack for young people, which included stationery and pre-stamped envelopes. Today such a pack might include phone cards or access to the internet. To this could be added brochures and photographs of the home and, at a later stage, photographs of the resident taken at the home. Some places make arrangements to meet buses or trains for visitors or have facilities in the home for people to stay.

There are many statements made about the importance of partnership between relatives and residents. Yet such partnership is very difficult to achieve. Relatives are no longer clear as to their role as caring relative. Probably they do not know what they can do nor the responsibilities that they can take. If we are to get beyond glib statements of relatives being welcomed, there has to be analysis.

First, there needs to be understanding of the relationships before the resident moved in: how did people perceive others? what did they do for each other?

Second, given these relationships, what involvement should relatives play in the preparation for a move? Relatives will have knowledge of the resident-to-be: their likes and dislikes; their hopes and fears; what they can and cannot manage. Of course, the prospective residents themselves will have very thorough knowledge of the same factors.

Finally, there is the aspect of continuing contact between relative and resident. Relatives are no longer clear as to their role. Their former responsibility has been reduced and their continuing responsibility has to be negotiated. The relatives' role in the home is no longer defined.

One aspect is often little understood by staff: relatives find it hard to maintain contact because the activity of visiting without a role is strange. One mother described visiting her son:

> The point is that you don't really know what to do. All the sort of things I normally did with David didn't seem normal any more... You couldn't do that in front of people you don't know... You know I used to think about buses and things, but I don't think they (the staff) ever believed me. I reckon it was all going down in some black book somewhere... I just felt lonely and useless and no one would tell me anything. (Millham *et al.*, 1986, p. 138)

A cluster of factors comes together: there are practical difficulties for people in visiting; they may feel that staff are checking on how good they are as relatives; they do not know what to do when they visit; they may sense that their role has been taken away. This is akin to friends visiting patients in hospital, parents visiting children in boarding schools or separated parents taking their children out: how is the event to be managed? what do we do? how can we be together in a way which allows some chance for sharing feelings? In any of this thinking, the changed relationship of the relative or friend to the resident has to be managed: visitors may well have passed to the home some of the previous caring responsibilities, about which they have mixed feelings.

The position is more complicated when the perspective of other parties is introduced. Residents may not want to see relatives, may not want relatives to do things for them, may be uneasy as to the reasons for the visit or angry about past tensions in relationships. Staff may feel relatives' visit as intrusive, as if relatives are checking up on the staff care. One response to this is to try to exclude relatives from doing things for the residents by making it clear that it is the staff task to do and to take responsibility for the caring: 'What if the resident falls when a relative is taking her to the lavatory?' staff may think.

> The relative said to me (senior staff member) 'I'll just take Mum off for a wash, she's a bit smelly.' Then she saw my face. 'Well if you don't mind' she added. 'I'm sorry, I do. It's our responsibility and I've got plenty of staff to do it.' We've had trouble with visitors like that. I don't mind them doing some things but not things that are our job. *Our girls would wonder why other people were doing their work*. (Clough, 1981, p. 147)

Further dimensions are introduced when we recognize that motivations are not always straightforward or easily understood. I have known staff in homes for adults who were convinced that relatives were only coming to collect money from the resident. In such circumstances it is essential to reinforce the perspective of residents as adults with rights to choose what they do with their own money. Yet, if they have not enough for their own use or feel under pressure to give their money away, they may need some protection.

A final factor to consider in preparation for a new resident is the other people already in the home, the residents and staff. How are they to be involved in the arrangements?

The structuring of residential living

Knowledge of the components of good practice has to be used to construct the sort of satisfactory arrangements for living that we all want in our homes: comfort, security, safety, space, acceptance. The new place of living, the residential home, must be a good enough place to live. This does not just come about. It has to be created: argued, perhaps fought over; negotiated; and constructed.

What happens in a residential home has to be, in current management terms, fit for purpose: the structures and processes should lead to the objectives of the establishment being realized. Residents differ in terms of life-stage, shown in their interests and capacities but also in what they feel they have to manage. Each person is managing past, present and future: some residents will be young with a presumption that most of life is unlived; others will be old, with most of life in their past. Staff in residential homes need to think about the way structures and processes can allow and support such review, with its potential refocus of energy. The lifestyle created within a residential home has to support people in managing these life-stages. In the end, people have to manage for themselves: others cannot determine or resolve my feelings about myself. Life in the home has to be planned in such a way that people can live full lives in physical, spiritual and psychological terms.

It is obvious that residential life is about *living*, but an analysis of tasks which breaks down the activities into parts can distort this. Thus people may focus on *rights* or *choice*, and neglect the fundamental that residence should offer the opportunity to develop one's life. The test of the adequacy of structures and processes has to be this larger and more nebulous one of 'opportunity to develop one's life'. That is not to deny the importance of either rights or choices, as important components of good practice and ones that should be used as indicators of performance. But the fundamental is how people feel about themselves in the place where they live.

The link between skills, activities and inner state is vital. Residents of homes, young or old, may need direct, physical help to get dressed or to join in activities. However, they may have lost confidence in any of a number of ways: in being able to learn, in meeting people or, indeed, in themselves as worthwhile people. Consequently, they may have given up doing things for themselves, getting to know other people or taking any initiative in planning. There is a danger of treating residents as passive, rather than as people who, with support, can develop or recover a capacity to take control of parts of their lives.

6

An Ethical Base for Practice

Introduction

In a residential home there are numerous occasions on which people have to work out what to do. In doing so, they exercise judgement. What is the basis on which such decisions are taken?

Two examples from a study of children's homes illustrate this:

> A newcomer refused to attend school. Other young people said, 'If he is not attending school, why should we have to?' Soon three young people refused to attend.

> Virtually the whole group persecuted one boy, tying his clothes into knots, hiding his toothbrush, etc. (Whitaker *et al.*, 1998, pp. 70–1)

How do staff work out what to do about the non-attendance at school? Are there values which help to clarify action? The second example raises different questions. There is no doubt that the behaviour of the group towards the one boy is not acceptable, although there may be reasons for their annoyance with him. What is to happen?

More scenarios could be added to introduce further dilemmas. Two adult residents might be in dispute because they disagree over which programme to watch on the television, the behaviour of one is intrusive on another, or one person's conversation is perceived as hurtful by another. What should staff do?

Cain (1998) posits other dilemmas:

> a boy was required to leave (a home) because he was judged to be a leader in sexual abuse: other children wanted, perhaps needed, to know why he'd left. To tell them would be a breach of confidentiality and so not 'discreet' – but would it be beneficial?... a worker was offered promotion which meant he would have to break off a fruitful therapeutic relationship with a boy: should this be seen as a lack of loyalty and, if so, would it be justifiable? (p. 130)

From beliefs to practice

The question 'What *ought* workers to do?' faces us with the test of values. Further brief scenarios highlight potential dilemmas as to action: someone is incontinent at night-time; a person wants to break links with family; a resident repeatedly annoys other residents, perhaps poking them with a walking stick when walking around the home or preventing someone from watching a favourite TV programme in peace; another individual does not keep to the rules or expectations; someone else is unhappy and is reluctant to come out of a bedroom; another resident talks of suicide; or a person is physically and verbally abusive to staff. How are beliefs and values of use in helping us think what to do? I aim to illustrate ways of thinking about the practical implementation of beliefs and values rather than to produce a compendium of values in action.

A study of the British Association of Social Workers' (BASW) *Code of Ethics for Social Work* illustrates ways of trying to move from principle to practice (Watson, 1985). The code starts with a statement of principles, the first of which reads:

> Basic to the profession of social work is the recognition of the value and dignity of every human being, irrespective of origin, status, sex, sexual orientation, age, belief or contribution to society. The profession accepts a responsibility to encourage and facilitate the self-realization of the individual person with due regard for the interest of others. (Quoted in Watson, 1985, p. 2)

Watson makes the point that the first sentence, recognizing the value of every human being, should not and cannot be claimed as exclusive to social work but that that does not make the statement inappropriate (p. 21). He goes on to state that although the first half of that sentence is at a high level of abstraction, it is made specific in statements 'of what does *not* detract from the value and dignity of a human being'. Critics fear, he argues, not that a statement in such abstract terms cannot be applied to practice but that it is 'capable of application in *a number* of ways' (original emphasis, p. 31).

The code lists consequent obligations on the worker:

> He will contribute to the formulation and implementation of policies for human welfare...
>
> He will respect... clients as individuals...
>
> He will not act selectively towards clients out of prejudice...
>
> He will help... clients increase the range of choices...

He will not reject his client or lose concern for his suffering, even if obliged to protect others against him...

He will give precedence to his professional responsibility over his personal interests. (quoted in Watson, 1985, p. 3)

In later chapters authors examine the implications of trying to put such a code into effect. Payne (1985) claims that the code is of limited use in resolving tensions between the interests of client and agency and needs further elaboration. Similarly, Hudson (1985, p. 145) points out tensions for a manager. Do these obligations encompass: the children admitted to the home; those not admitted; neighbours; management bodies? He shows also the way in which the behaviour of a resident can be judged as deviant: staff may try to stop from going out an elderly man who walks out of a home to look for his deceased wife, wanting to help him settle in his new surroundings (p. 146).

In *Residential Work* I argued the case for specifying the rights of residents. The essence of the argument is that staff have immense power over the daily lives of residents: staff interpret what are the needs, wants and interests of residents; staff have far more information than residents about what can be done; staff provide services which residents need. One way to transfer some of this power is to clarify what residents have a right to expect. Indeed, such clarity would help to prevent abuse. I am struck by the continuing relevance of a particular example:

An old lady did not do as she was told by a staff member in one home I visited. As a result she was told to go to bed and, when she did not, she was carried to bed by a staff member. (Clough, 1982, p. 107)

Ten years later, when working in an inspection unit, we found that a proprietor carried residents to bed when they did not go to bed at a prescribed time.

'The fundamental right', I stated, 'is for the resident, plus relative or friend, to have a say in planning for her own life'.

For the resident the issue is the same as that which exists for all of us: to find a way of caring for self *and* caring for others; to promote self-interest while protecting the rights of others; to find a *method* of achieving those goals which is morally acceptable. (Clough, 1982, p. 109)

Such general statements have to be interpreted in individual circumstances. Specific statements may not deal with related but differing events. What if a staff member forcibly persuades people to go to bed when they do not want to, rather than carries them to bed? So general statements of rights are useful. However, neither statements of rights nor codes of practice can remove the judgement of the worker and the judgement of the resident. Each situation differs from any other. There will be many similarities between undertaking the same task with different people at different times but there will also be significant variations, such as when a resident who is smelly does not want to wash, when a person is very upset or frightened, or when someone is violent towards the staff member. In other words the guidance is general and has to be interpreted on each individual occasion. Because of the nature of residential work it is essential that there is this freedom to interpret because otherwise staff are rule bound and provide standardized, but ultimately, sterile care.

There is no easy route from the specification of a principle to action. We may *know* that the action we want to take *should* be predicated, as in the *Code of Ethics* above, on a belief in 'the recognition of the value and dignity of every human being' and may *want* to act in such a way. Yet it is still difficult to work out what to do when a resident is aggressive towards others or refuses to wash. The best outcome can only be achieved through a struggle to work out what is best, bearing in mind the value and dignity of this resident, of other residents and of staff. I interpret their value to be something which they retain unchanged whatever their behaviour, social circumstances or economic value.

Recognizing 'the value and dignity of every human being' differs from politeness. It is an active state in which others are taken seriously; workers strive to understand; they do not patronize. The process of 'striving to understand' is important in itself for it shows that we are concerned for others. *Listening* is correctly listed as one of the core attributes in communication. But we all know the different ways in which we and others listen:

- with half an ear, or less, while concentrating on something else; this may involve using the words which would suggest that we are thinking about what someone has said when we are giving it little attention;

- using or allowing the events described to stimulate our thinking about ourselves;

- by contrast, the times when someone gives their concentrated attention to another are apparent because their attention is focused and they pursue the 'story' to get clarification or development.

I would contend that to act in accord with a belief in 'the recognition of the value and dignity of every human being', demands that the individual's perception of their identity is included. It is tempting – but dangerous – to presume that from our own experience we can know what someone else thinks or wants. There are numerous examples of practices built on stereotypes and, typically, we are unlikely to see our own sets of beliefs as stereotypes.

Assumptions are made about others: of older people, perhaps that they are not capable of, nor interested in, learning; that people are heterosexual, thus denying homosexual people the chance to be open in their relationships; of different ethnic groups, that they have more ability for certain jobs than others; that people with disabilities should be grateful for the services they receive; or of women, that they will perform the maintenance tasks of making the tea and washing up.

Values and professions

Many professions produce ethical codes such as BASW's already cited. In medicine, the focus of the Hippocratic oath has been on the relationship between doctor and patient. Biestek in the 1960s, writing about social work, described the essential, fundamental attitude of social workers towards clients as 'respect for persons'. Butrym's (1976) writing is one of the best discussions of Biestek's approach, linked to a wider consideration of the nature of social work and of social work values. She sets out Biestek's core values:

- acceptance
- non-judgemental attitude
- individualization
- purposeful expression of feelings
- controlled emotional involvement
- confidentiality
- self-determination.

The starting point of Butrym is that:

Social work derives from society of which it is a part... The preoccupation of social work with people and their social circumstances creates its main occupational risk – a lack of specificity, an inherent ambiguity. (p. ix)

Thus, she counters a weakness in Biestek that his stance led to an acceptance of social injustices arising from structural factors. Similarly, it is impossible properly to understand values for residential work divorced from, first, society's values, second, the function society wants residential workers to fulfil and, third, the function that residential workers claim to be fulfilling. Residential workers, as other social workers, have to consider whether it is part of their work to change external conditions and structures and help people to challenge, rather than adjust to, intolerable situations.

The recognition of the impact of social circumstances on individuals has been one of the main contributions the discipline of social work has made to other professions' understanding of people's behaviour. An example of this is seen in the shift away from interpreting mental illness solely as a medical problem. Social work has also been in the forefront of highlighting the structural disadvantage and discrimination faced by different groups, and of demanding that social workers challenge such discrimination. Thus the Central Council for Education in Social Work (CCETSW) requires that students know about:

> Sources and forms of oppression, disadvantage and discrimination based on: race, gender, religion, language, age, class, disability and being gay and lesbian, their impact at a structural and individual level, and strategies and actions to deal with them. (CCETSW, 1995)

A social worker is expected to 'identify, analyse and take action to counter discrimination, racism, disadvantage, inequality and injustice, using strategies appropriate to role and context'.

CCETSW requires that social workers, including residential workers, should study and be competent in terms of knowledge, skills and values. The statement is sound. The dangers, in particular in relation to values, are that the values professed may not be put into practice and that they may be difficult to interpret in a specific situation.

Specification and nature of values

What then is meant by 'values'?

> Values are things we value. They are modern terminology for talking about what is 'good'. In ethical theory it is moral value in which we are interested, but there are other types of value such as economic, aesthetic or functional. We value

things economically in terms of what their exchange value is, be they bushels of corn or paintings by Picasso. Clearly the economic value of a thing depends on what people will pay for it, or how much they desire it. In other words, economic value is subjective: a Picasso painting is not worth a fixed price but is worth what people will pay. If we turn to aesthetic value, this is less clear: is a painting 'good' only because lots of people think so, or are there standards for what makes paintings good that experts can apply independent of popular vote?

Functional value is less subjective: it seems we can agree on fairly objective standards for what makes a knife or lawnmower 'good' or fit for their purpose. (David Clough, personal communication 1997)

The values which are being referred to when there is mention of 'values in residential work' are moral values. Are these thought of as absolute or relative, objective or subjective? The questions raise practical not just abstract matters. They face us with the reality of what words mean.

Various writers use words such as 'objectives', 'governing principles' and 'values' to describe a combination of what should be the aims of residential care together with the process by which such aims are to be achieved.

Burton (1998, p. 98) writes that 'the accepted values of residential care are embodied in the description of residents' entitlements set out and defined in *Homes are for Living in*':

Privacy: the right of individuals to be left alone or undisturbed and free from intrusion or public attention into their affairs.

Dignity: recognition of the intrinsic value of people regardless of circumstances by respecting their uniqueness and their personal needs; treating with respect.

Independence: opportunities to act and think without reference to another person, including a willingness to incur a degree of calculated risk.

Choice: opportunity to select independently from a range of options.

Rights: the maintenance of entitlements associated with citizenship.

Fulfilment: the realization of personal aspirations and abilities in all aspects of daily life. (DoH, 1989)

The Residential Forum (1996, p. 19) contends that, 'Principles apply to all Homes and should underpin all aspects of life in them.' One of these principles is that residents should be able to enjoy 'a preferred way of life':

[This principle] touches in some way all the underlying principles of good quality care. [It] includes the exercise of rights and risks, making choices and being

enabled to be independent. It means respecting individuality and being treated
with dignity. It also involves enabling self-determination and the opportunity to
have fulfilling experiences. (p. 39)

One means of trying to understand the ethical base of practice in residential work is to demand precision in language. Moral philosophers do
just this and claim that an analysis of meaning will help to clarify not
just meaning but action. Hare (1978) states that the problems on which
moral philosophy 'tries to shed light are practical issues about
morality'. He asks: 'How could you decide what was a fair pay rise... if
you had no idea what "fair" meant, and therefore no idea what would
settle such questions?' (p. 152). He distinguishes facts from values:
facts are statements of what is, values raise the question of 'ought'.

Hare uses fairness as an example of a term that has to be examined
for its meaning. It is easy for all of us to state that we believe in 'fair
pay rises' and probably most of us would subscribe to such a statement.
It is only when we pursue what we each mean by fairness that this
unexceptionable statement becomes fought-over territory. Does 'fairness' mean maintenance of differentials, less for the rich, more for those
who work harder, have had less opportunity, or who tackle unpleasant
jobs? Should I get paid less if I enjoy my work than if I do not?

In the same way we can debate the sorts of opportunities which
should be available to the troubled and troublesome young people who
live in residential homes. To take a recent controversy, is it 'fair' that
they might go on adventure training exercises to which other young
people might not have access?

Similarly, we need to check whether there is shared meaning of words
that are readily used in residential work such as *dignity* or *privacy*.

Authors have focused on three aspects of values in residential work:

1. *attributes or principles judged necessary for 'good living'*
   ('independence', 'choice' and so on),
2. *people's rights* (for example, 'to be able to participate as a full
   citizen'),
3. *what workers should not do* ('they should not discriminate').

There is much less written on what are the fundamental, positive
values that should underpin workers' practice.

There is a great difference in ethics between *rules* and *laws*, on the one hand, and
virtues on the other. Rules often say what I must not do, and are absolute: mostly
they just set the external limits within which the situation is so complicated that no

simple rules can be laid down. Virtues, on the other hand, are patterns of behaviour, of which typical examples can be given: for example, they can be illustrated
in stories; they tend to be associated with words like 'character'; and they tend to
be positive rather than negative. (J. Fletcher, personal communication 1997)

If the notion of 'values in practice' is to have any currency it must
relate to helping workers to think about what they should do. An assertion that 'residential work should have an ethical base', makes sense
only if residential work is a morally good activity.

An ethical base for practice

Residential work is about doing: the purpose of the work is to produce
services and activities that are wanted and needed by residents. In
effect, the work must be purposeful, that is directed to an end. In
carrying out the work, staff make judgements as to *what* is to be done
and *how* it is to be done. The fact that the manner in which something
is done, that is the process, is an important part of the service itself
must not lead to a presumption that the process is all that matters. In a
doctor I want both what we call 'a good bedside manner' (someone
who listens, gives me time and thinks about my concerns) but also
someone with technical skill. Similarly, writing about social work,
Sainsbury *et al.* (1982) wrote:

> Our impression is that while there can be no effective social work without a
> 'good' relationship – for clients frequently judge the quality of the work by refer-
> ence to the personal attributes of their worker in terms of relationships – relation-
> ship is rarely enough in itself to enhance the ability of clients to resolve their
> problems. (p. 190)

Studies of residential work increasingly have focused on outcome:
what is the result of what is done? There may be debates as to what the
outcomes of residential care should be, and about how such outcomes
should be measured, but there is agreement that we have to find ways
to describe what are the consequences of living in a residential home.
Whitaker *et al.* (1998) note that it is possible to state desired
outcomes when a young person enters a home. These may be specific
or general, short or long term, intermediate or final. Some outcomes are
marked by 'easily observable events': 'a young person is back at
school, or not, or has spent a week-end at home without getting into
another violent encounter with a parent' (p. 196). They recognize also

that it is not easy to identify what leads to successful or unsuccessful outcomes. For example, a former young person from a children's home, meeting the manager of the home in the street, says, 'You did well by me.' Was he lucky or was he helped? Other research has acknowledged the significance to outcome of events which are outside the parameters of the establishment, in particular what happens within the young person's family or network.

It is here that the link must be made with ethics. I contend that some styles of living alongside others are better than others and that this becomes of greater significance when people are damaged, vulnerable, troubled or troublesome. Thus the living experience is something which to is be examined in its own right. It will never be possible to be certain that one event in a home leads to a particular outcome. We should not claim that the way in which a staff member helped someone get to bed at night was *necessarily* the reason why a resident had a better night. The staff member's actions are important; they are likely to have an impact on the resident but the sleep pattern may be affected also by what someone has had to eat or drink, by whether they have had exercise or by other residents. Residential work is not an exact science in which we can show causal links.

Yet it is vital that, without knowing the precise impact of their work, staff recognize its importance. Some styles of looking after other people (or caring or helping, whatever terms are thought acceptable) are better than others. The creation of a good place to live is an outcome in its own right. And it is imperative that residential homes recognize the value and dignity of residents even when staff may feel powerless to help someone get beyond their depression or hurt.

So the starting point to a consideration of ethics in relation to residential care is to examine whether the activity of providing residential care can be morally good. If residential homes are harmful, they should not be in existence. This is a serious point given that some people's analysis of residential homes has placed them as poor alternatives to other lifestyles and that there is growing awareness of abuse and malpractice. Running residential homes cannot be justified unless, given the circumstances in which prospective residents find themselves, homes are thought to be good places to live.

This is the equivalent of acknowledging that, in a pluralistic society, there are different acceptable ways to bring up children. However, some ways are considered unacceptable. Residential homes should not exist unless they are regarded as one acceptable way of providing housing and care for the people who live in them. Earlier I noted the former optimism that the environment of a residential home could be used to benefit a resident. Today, sobered by the recognition that while some people have benefited from residential life, others have led restricted lives and, worse, been assaulted in homes, far fewer claims would be made about the beneficence of residential living. Neverthe- less, I contend that residential homes should not exist unless there is an optimism that the work they do has importance and value for the lives of residents.

Residential homes differ one from another as well as having similar- ities, and so there are dangers in making general statements. All exist in a climate in which they are nearer a last resort than a first choice. Some have the task of looking after people for whom there is little idea of what can be done. This is particularly the case with some disturbed young people but may apply to some adults: possibly people with dementia who are violent and unhappy or those with severe learning disabilities who are aggressive towards themselves and others. Recog- nizing that for some residents, there is very little idea of how to help or even contain does away with the picture of cosy care which should be able to transform anybody's life. Hard-headed reality is imperative to sound provision of residential care.

Recently, I have reread Balbernie's foreword to *After Grace – Teeth*, (1975, pp. xiii–xxix), a study of approved schools for young people whom today we would term 'troubled and troublesome'. As head of the Cotswold Community, he was at the centre of the shift from approved school to therapeutic community. I am impressed by his realism coupled with a passionate belief as to the importance of the quality of residential care.

He suggests that by 1960 approved schools 'had in the main lost heart'... 'There was no real enjoyment or well-being left' (p. xiv). The schools easily became 'dustbins', into which society offloaded its rejects; they were given 'an impossible task', a fact that could be used as a defence for failing to do anything: 'What can you expect us to do?', they could argue, 'given the confusion of task and young people, the lack of resources' and so on. It is possible to create homes in which there is superficial order but the real selves of the young people are untouched. By contrast, Balbernie contends: 'We can do very little, if anything, for such a high proportion of these severely damaged young people. This is not the same as saying that we can do nothing' (p. xxvii). He is dismissive of attempts to gloss over the disturbance of the young people. Two sides of his reality, what Lyward might have called 'stern love' (Burn, 1967), are evident in these statements:

This study is about those very nasty and empty young people who persistently steal and who yet prick our social consciences and who make us feel so passionately furious or sentimental in living with them. Their despair is profound; they are sad and without hope.

These are young people, many of whom have been devalued, degraded and depersonalized since birth. (Balbernie, 1975, pp. xvii–xviii)

The points about realism, clarity of task and support for the primary task relate to all types of residential homes. Miller and Gwynne (1972) discussed understandings of disability and the implications for models of residential practice. Those models which focused only on growth and development, the 'horticultural', laudable as they were in many ways, failed to recognize that some people were becoming physically more frail. Emphasizing the importance of growth, could make residents (and, potentially, staff) feel failures if they could not develop new skills.

From all of this we can compile a number of questions about residential homes:

- Is there a real understanding of the nature of the task which a home is to undertake?
- Has the style of the home been developed to deal with the real task?
- Are there adequate resources, in particular people and buildings, to do the task well enough?
- Do staff retain a belief in the value of their work?

If managers and staff cannot answer 'Yes' to these questions, then the residential home should not be allowed to continue. Ideally, in some way the wider society should also be approving the practice. Staff have to decide whether to continue to work in settings which they believe are harmful. My argument has been that in considering values in residential work we have to start with whether the activity of residential care is morally good. The real nature of the task must be understood and, recognizing the limits to what is possible, a lifestyle must be created which is satisfactory.

The task created is impossible, and set to fail, unless there is recognition of the impact of residents' former lives, their current social structures outside the home and their inner state. Residential care cannot solve all the problems of an individual. Given current knowledge, some situations appear almost intractable: the 'healing' or 'the making whole' that might be desired may be unachievable. Nevertheless the lifestyle created can demonstrate the worth and value of the resident.

Indeed, the point made earlier that the provision of good experience is worthwhile, has relevance here: in residential care people must be looked after in ways which provide such good experiences.

Who sets the values?

Different groups of people have an interest in what happens in residential homes: most importantly the resident, but also staff, relatives, purchasers (if the resident is not the purchaser), internal and external managers, and inspectors. The list could be extended by including councillors (with responsibility for social services directly provided services, including assessment and purchase), visiting professionals (social workers, nurses, doctors, physio- and occupational therapists), advocates, volunteers, neighbours and local community. Each of these has different interests and responsibilities.

These various categories of people have, as stated, *an interest* in what happens. But how is the life of the place determined? Each of these groups will have different abilities to assert their view and, within each group, some individuals, similarly, will have a greater ability to implement what they think than others. However, it is also useful to look at what are the influential factors in the construction of life in a residential home.

Much of residential life can be seen as a number of separate interactions or events between individuals: resident to resident, resident to staff member, staff member to staff member. Sometimes these are in private, sometimes semi-public, in that others are around. On many occasions there are several people involved in fluid groupings. Whether explicit or not, people will have an idea of what they think should be happening but, because of the complexity involved in any interaction, may find it difficult to define. Thus there may be ready agreement that people should be treated with respect: but do we all understand the same thing by the word 'respect'? Will there not be variations in understanding dependent on culture, socio-economic group, gender and sexual orientation? Further, even if we could create complete understanding and agreement on the meaning of 'respect', we would find differences in the interpretation of what happened as to whether or not an episode could be classified as respectful. Does this mean that examining values is pointless?

'Shared values' and 'culture' have been two terms by which authors have tried to describe the distinctive characteristics of residential homes. To gauge the extent to which various stakeholders have similar perceptions about objectives or style of life, researchers may get people to describe the key factors that typify the way the place works. There are various ways to do this. People may be asked: to tell stories which capture the essence of the place; to say how they would respond to a given situation; or to set out key characteristics. Of course observation and other methods can be used. What such methods attempt to do is to consider whether it is possible to describe a culture and, second, the extent of sharing in that culture.

Analysis such as this can be undertaken also in prospect. 'How do we want people to live in this home?' is a question that could be asked of different interest groups. To what extent are decisions about lifestyle to be left to individuals?

Whitaker *et al.* (1998, p. 2) define culture as 'the values, norms, shared beliefs, assumptions and expectations held by a social group, roles and role differentiation, and characteristic interactive patterns and styles'. They note that some aspects of culture can be seen, while others are implicit. Of course different groups, and within them sub-groups, may have cultures of their own. The resident culture may differ from that of the staff. Or the internal culture (that of the residents and staff) may be at variance with outsiders, as might happen if an accident resulted in the death of an adult resident. Insiders might see this as sad, but the result of an agreed policy that residents can bath themselves, go out on their own or participate in outdoor pursuits. Outsiders might view this as neglect. Alternatively, with young people, it may be thought by those outside the home that the resident is having too good a time (facilities or holidays are too lavish): 'We thought they were there to be... educated or punished or looked after, not given a holiday', runs the argument. It is also useful to note that cultures are not static (Brown *et al.*, 1998).

The study of culture is a means of describing distinctive characteristics. It should be seen as a useful term for understanding residential life, but is not a complete answer to describing difference, similarity and cohesion.

There is a debate as to whether or not it is useful to talk of 'culture': the word 'culture' may lead to a presumption that there are definable common and shared experiences. One school of thought would argue that the individuals who live and work in a home are so different that the focus should be on their differences, not on the small amount that is in common. (Clough, 1996b, p. 59)

Further, the existence of a coherent culture does not mean practice is good.

> The topic is of fundamental importance for two reasons. The first is that homes may become too focused on their internal worlds. The second, important for a different reason, is that strong culture establishments have at times been abusive establishments. We have learnt to our cost in the UK that some places where there is a pervasive culture – and where outsiders find it difficult to find their way in – may be harmful to children. There are examples of establishments where insiders were discouraged from asking questions and outsiders were persuaded that they did not know enough to question a strong leader. (Clough, 1996b, pp. 65–6)

A belief system is an overarching collection of ideas which is explanatory on different levels: individual, social and cosmic (Magee, 1978, p. 52). Such belief systems are likely to be most comprehensive if they arise from a religion, philosophy or ideology, in the sense of a system of ideas. Many people – and many residential homes – do not have coherent belief systems. We have more of a ragbag of beliefs. But beliefs are of a higher conceptual order than values, which can be understood as the precepts by which we try to live out our beliefs. Ward (1998) writes that one of many characteristics of therapeutic communities for young people is 'the use of psychodynamic rather than solely behavioural or cognitive theoretical frameworks to underpin the treatment philosophy' (p. 65). Not all residential homes will have as clear an approach. However, I suggest that all should endeavour to create a coherent theoretical framework.

Beliefs in action

Let us take an example of a young person or an adult who wets their bed. How is this to be understood? What is to be done? With children, one approach might be based on a view that they are likely to stop wetting their beds at some stage, that those who have faced disturbance might be prone to revert to younger behaviour and that the best way to deal with the matter is to minimize the anxiety of young person and staff: 'You will stop wetting your bed soon and the less you worry about it the better.' Staff would work out with the young person how to manage being wet and washing as discreetly as possible.

Alternatively, there may be a view that management of food or drink may help: the person is encouraged not to drink large quantities of fluid after a certain time and to avoid particular foods or drinks that stimulate the bladder; in addition, in particular with an adult, there would be a review of the side effects of medication.

Yet another approach would be to consider illness or disease: there are many conditions which lead to temporary incontinence. There are also permanent conditions such as muscle weakness in women and enlarged prostate glands in men which can result in incontinence. Changes to the nervous system, in particular with dementia, may result in an inability to control one's bladder. Surgical and medical approaches may be considered.

A behavioural approach would assert that people can learn to deal with the symptoms and control the behaviour. Rewards might be given as reinforcers of desired behaviour. There have been methods in which children have been wakened by mild electrical stimuli when they have wet the bed, so that they would not get used to lying in warm, wet bedclothes.

Any diagnosis or treatment has to be informed by a theoretical framework, tested against a belief system and evaluated. We know that treatment for medical conditions may at times be counter-intuitive, in that what works goes against our presumptions. Indeed, frequently treatment is painful and demands that patients put themselves in situations which we associate with indignities. Yet, if we value the treatment, we put up with the pain and the indignities, although, hopefully, medical staff endeavour to reduce both. The treatment can be regarded as ethically good.

Let me examine how this analysis might be applied to dealing with incontinence of young people. One approach might take the form of the young people having to wash sheets in front of other young people. Instinctively, I dislike this as it appears to demean the young person. However, it is important to examine the basis for such views.

The approach might be based on ideas that have not been thought through; when asked to reconsider the method, staff decide that it is not good practice. However, the practice might be based on a theoretical framework in which bed-wetting is seen as learnt behaviour that can be modified by reward of desired behaviour and sanctions against undesired behaviour. (Another school of thought might choose to ignore, and so extinguish, the unwanted behaviour.)

My dislike of shaming of children who wet their beds is based on a value as to what constitutes people's worth, and the importance for people of maintaining their self-esteem. As long as there are approaches which are at least as effective as any claimed for shaming, then it is reasonable for me to hold on to a coherence between beliefs, values and theoretical framework – and to reject the shaming. However, if it were to happen that research claimed shaming to be a more effective way of dealing with some children's bed-wetting, and, indeed, that children were happier after the shaming because they were continent, then I ought to re-examine the basis of my ideas. What is it in my beliefs, values or theoretical framework which questions shaming? Should I amend any one of these?

Of course, the notion of 'successful outcome' must not be allowed free rein. We know that some medical treatments which were hailed as successful at the time have turned out to have devastating side effects. The best we can do is to test rigorously the theory in its own right and then to examine it against our beliefs. We should then explain the reasons for our judgement, which allows others to understand and question our position.

If staff understand and agree with the stated values, they will use those values as a way of determining how they should work. The maxim of St Augustine, 'Love God and do what you will', is premised on the assumption that if you love God, what you will like to do will be what is good. Similarly, this emphasis on values is not a recipe for anything being acceptable. The more that staff are in harmony with the values of the organization, the more they can be left free to be creative and to interpret what they will do.

Peters and Waterman (1982), writing about successful organizations, place shared values as the key variable. Books on residential practice have long recognized the importance of shared values: see Wolins (1974); Clough (1982, 1991) or, recently, Brown *et al.* (1998) and Whitaker *et al.* (1998).

In a wider framework, Millham *et al.* (1975a) argue that the more different interest groups agree as to task and objective for residential work, the more chance there is of success. 'Shared values' needs to extend outside the residential home. They argue that the approved schools they were studying were more successful when key parties shared expectations. In some writing on residential work there is an awareness of a different dimension: the impact of the values of the residents. At times this has been referred to as 'sub-culture', in particular when the resident values run counter to the professed values of the organization.

A general point emerges from this: to write of values as if they are the sole domain of staff or management distorts life in a residential home. How far should the belief system, theoretical framework and values be negotiated between residents and staff? In fact the response to the question must vary with different types of establishment and with whether or not the place is long established. Thus a therapeutic community for young people or adults might have an established theoretical framework: the way in which that is implemented in day-to-day life may be subject to negotiation with residents, taking account of their capacity to participate in such discussions. It is always likely that the theoretical framework will be more influenced by the workers, who should have a greater grasp of the theory. Nevertheless, people in a local community may see the results of a theoretical approach and want to establish such an establishment, as has happened on many occasions with hospices. People may also want to set up a home which caters for central aspects of their own belief system. A TV documentary recently showed people of Asian origin looking for a residential home. They wanted somewhere that would allow their elders to live as they wanted, in particular to be able to practise their religion. Most homes they visited were not aware of what they would want, although some were willing to try to adapt aspects of their lifestyle. They were not looking for a particular theoretical framework so much as a real understanding of their religion, language and culture.

Reflecting on values from earlier times

In the second half of the nineteenth century Barnardo was one of several people who set up residential homes for children. Rudolf's work led to the foundation of the Church of England Children's Society, Stephenson's to the National Children Homes and there were many smaller groups such as the Mueller Homes around Bristol. These individuals would have said that their work sprang from their religion or philanthropy, a concern for the well-being of the children who had no homes or who were living rough on the streets. The residential homes to which they went were to care for and protect them, and to offer them some form of education and training.

Barnardo wrote over the doorway of his residential home that no destitute child was ever turned away. We can examine the principles on which the home was based in a number of ways:

- in terms of the experiences of the children at that time: life inside the residential home compared to life outside;
- by considering the motivation of Barnardo and those working within the home;
- the outcome for the children of living in the home.

For example, some people would argue that whatever else was intended the home fulfilled the function for society of taking seemingly dangerous children off the streets and training them for work activities in which there was a shortage of labour, such as domestic service and agriculture. In the process sometimes children travelled long distances from the places where they had lived. Indeed some were sent abroad. It is probably accurate to state that the prevalent belief, at least in the middle classes, was that the potential advantages of being brought up in a middle-class family outweighed the disadvantages of moving away from one's peers.

Today we know that the certainty that such moves were to the advantage of the child at times led to children being moved with insufficient consultation with parents and even against their wishes. We know too that children were taken from the UK for adoption in Australia and Canada, in effect a type of transportation, right up to the 1950s.

The people involved in such placements are likely to have said that they had the welfare of the child at the centre of their practice. Terms like this one of 'the welfare of the child at the heart of policy and practice' trip off the tongue easily; but they also capture an essential of good child care practice. Unless the complexity of the term is examined, together with the recognition that there may be conflicting aspects of welfare, what is so readily termed 'a value base' may be empty words. If the idea that basing one's work on values is of any use in practice, the values must be specified and debated.

Another dimension is that if we reflect today about the past, it can seem as if, with the presumed wisdom of hindsight, every attempt to help others was flawed. We have to recognize that sometimes placing children in residential homes separated them from their parents in ways that rightly we question. We have to recognize also that many children had fuller and happier lives as the result of the residential care that was provided: without such homes many children would have died or led impoverished lives on the streets or in a workhouse. Many adults speak eloquently of the love and care they had from staff in children's homes. The fact that we judge to be wrong the placing of some children in residential homes should not lead to a dismissal of all residential care.

Morally good practice

The study of ethics in relation to residential work is both extremely complex and extremely important. People have tended to take sides in considering both whether residential homes are needed and whether they are fundamentally good or bad places. The reasons why their existence arouses such polarized feelings are uncertain but I suspect a part of the explanation is that they raise questions as to the best ways to house and care for people who are unable to manage on their own. These are not questions which touch the individual alone: they raise debates about the nature of parenting and of caring, the responsibility of family members and of society.

Perhaps what we should learn from reflection on the past is the dangers of certainty. We can be as arrogant today about current practice and about the failings of the past. However 'avoiding the dangers of certainty' must not lead to sloppy, unreasoned practice in which whims are collected to form an *ad hoc* lifestyle.

Current key terms

Certainty is often applied to terms in current usage. I shall in turn consider empowerment, dependency and interdependency, and self-esteem.

Empowerment

While I have noted the lack of power of residents, it is a mistake to present residents as powerless: studies of large residential establishments in the 1960s from prisons (Morris and Morris, 1963) to hospitals for people with learning disabilities (Morris, 1969) noted that the organizations could not function without the co-operation of the inmates. Nevertheless, residents are in a comparatively powerless position. The term 'empowerment' has immediate attractions for residential work. Stevenson (1996) writes forcefully:

> At the heart of the concept of empowerment is a moral assumption – that it is desirable to shift the balance of power... between worker and user. Indeed, the very endorsement of the ideal leads on to an articulation of rights, a process well illustrated at present in the field of disability. However, those on the side of the angels, enthusiasts for empowerment in social work, sometimes lack sophistication in formulating realistic goals and sensitive ways of working which take account of the individual's wishes and preoccupations, of their world view and of the limitations and constraints imposed by their characteristics. (p. 208)

In following this theme she highlights the context in which services are provided.

> Very old people, especially women, face a wide range of debilitating and frustrating conditions, which seriously limit mobility and/or social engagement. The taken-for-granted activities of adult life which create a sense of freedom and choice, integral to empowerment, are denied to many. (p. 209)

Given that so many old women live alone, she notes that 'they are deprived of ordinary opportunities for social stimulation'.

> Thus a central concern for social workers has to be how best to limit, control and remedy the effects of disability which so often is deeply disempowering. (p. 209)

The dilemma in trying to act in accord with oversimplified values or principle statements is caught when she confronts the difficulties facing workers who are 'sincerely committed to an empowering ideal'.

> In a process in which decline seems inevitable, the task and the problem which requires sensitive skill, is to preserve the opportunities for choice and decisions wherever possible but to recognize an equivalent moral duty to protect a vulnerable person. (p. 212)

The importance of the comment lies in the recognition that there are multiple principles and workers have to pursue several at the same time.

Dependency and interdependency

Independence is listed as a core value in many texts as in the earlier quotation where it was defined as 'opportunities to act and think without reference to another person, including a willingness to run a calculated risk' (DoH, 1989). The contrast is with dependency, the state of being dependent on another. Wilkin (1990), arguing that the focus on helplessness and powerlessness of many definitions is too restrictive, proposes that dependency be defined as: 'A state in which an individual *is reliant* upon other(s) for assistance in meeting *recognized needs.*' He creates a table in which causes of dependency are one variable: life-cycle; crisis; disablement; personality trait; socially/culturally defined (quoted in Johnson, 1993, pp. 258–9).

As Johnson states, 'If ways are to be found of reducing dependency, it is essential that causation is understood' (p. 260). In particular it would allow escape from designating people in blanket terms as 'dependent' or 'heavily dependent', which has implications for how that person is perceived in all areas of life. Thus a resident may be dependent on others for help at bath time: this might be to undress, to run the water, to get into the bath, to be looked after during the bath, to get out of the bath, to get dried or to get dressed. The person may need assistance in all these areas but may need help only in some.

Wilkin's definition also encourages thinking as to the extent to which dependency is socially or culturally defined. Are there aspects of residential life which create unwanted dependency? I remember a conversation with a resident who saw one of the staff go by with a pile of rags. 'That's the sort of thing I like doing', she said, 'cleaning up cupboards. If I stay in here long enough, I'll never walk. I could walk down to the shops at home.' A lot of the exercise people get occurs in the doing of necessary tasks. Does a move to a residential home make it more difficult and less likely that someone will continue to struggle to get dressed?

Dependency may be physical or emotional. It is probable that one of the main reasons why young people find it difficult to cope when they leave residential homes is related to emotional dependency. The focus of much effort has been on helping young people to develop life skills: cooking, budgeting, shopping and so on. Yet I suspect the far more difficult aspect of leaving a residential home is that of being alone. This demands a type of self-sufficiency which many adults find hard; many young people are protected in such moves to independence through living in accommodation with others such as student flats and by an ability to return home when they want. Is not some emotional dependency on other residents or staff in the home not only understandable but a mark of success? And, if so, what are the implications for moves out of a home?

Typically, dependency is viewed as negative. It is common for any of us to state that we do not want to be dependent on others. Yet, any of us may search for living arrangements with others in which there is considerable emotional dependency. Further, we are likely to enjoy being looked after. The parts of dependency that we do not like are when we are emotionally dependent on others whom we do not trust to have our welfare at heart or when we have to rely on others to do things for us because we cannot do them for ourselves. Dependency on others for some services is made easier if there is a measure of reciprocity. The reciprocity can be over a long period of time: an adult child may be happy to do things for a mother because 'She was always there when I wanted her.' Reciprocity does not need to be direct: we may be helped by some people and give help to others. Further, we can consider the relevance of 'interdependency' to life in residential homes.

Analysing dependency ensures that the nature of the dependency is examined. It is essential to distinguish aspects of a person's development and current state, in particular to distinguish their physical ageing from their psychological ageing. Physical ageing, in the sense of changes to the body and, consequently, to capacity to perform certain tasks, is an inevitability even though some people will nurture their bodies better than others. However, psychological ageing in the sense of capacity to learn and to manage oneself is different. People are able to bring experience to bear. Psychological ageing does not parallel physical ageing, although many adults with disabilities are treated as if it does.

Separating aspects of development is important also in understanding and working with children. Physical maturity may not have been matched by emotional maturity: young people's capacity for independence and for giving (and so for the reciprocity of interdependency) may be limited.

Dependency may also be created by structures: people with physical disability may have to get others to help because transport or access is poor; residents may have to ask for help with phoning because they do not have a phone in their room; rules or informal expectations may not allow people to do things for themselves. The recognition of the power inherent in providing services for others, and the powerlessness in not being able to decide when to do certain things without having to negotiate with staff, could lead staff to examine the ways in which services are provided. It is in this sort of analysis and debate that values are put into practice.

Self-esteem

Residents move into a residential home because they or others consider that they want or need support over and above that available to them at home. For the reasons discussed in earlier chapters, this overt recognition of 'need for support' tends to be seen as demeaning: we think more of ourselves if we can see ourselves as coping than not coping. A move to a residential home is thus a threat to a person's sense of self-worth. The self-esteem of family members may also be threatened.

It is essential to remember that a person's self-esteem is also likely to have been lowered by the events that precede the move into the home: an exclusion from school, being thrown out of your home, recognizing your inability to cope.

Coleman (1993) asks why some older people cope better with life's stresses than others. He notes that depression may be linked to low self-esteem. Factors that enhance coping are:

> a perception of being in control of events;
>
> positive self-worth: valuing self and seeing life as meaningful;
>
> having a confidant, which perhaps creates a sense of being valued and of reciprocal warmth;
>
> feeling positive about being cared for by others. (pp. 127–9)

Drawing on work by Sherman (1981) he suggests that 'older people need a way of feeling and thinking that allows them to be compassionate with themselves, and indeed, in the last analysis to transcend concern with themselves' (p. 130). How far is an analysis like this of use for thinking about children and younger adults? Given that our perception of self is in part built on our experiences of how we are treated, what can be done in a residential home to enhance residents' perception of self, of control of events, and of being cared for? Much of being looked after is resonant of how we were looked after in childhood, which was indicative of how others viewed us.

Challenging bad practice and developing good practice

Staff in residential homes will be faced with situations which they find problematic. They have to work out what they *should* do and what they *will* do. Of course, workers in any setting will at times face dilemmas as to correct practice. What is distinctive in residential work is that the lives of residents are influenced by the decisions which staff make. There are two types of tension which I shall examine briefly in the remainder of this chapter.

The first occurs when trying to work out how to respond to behaviour of residents that is in some way problematic. Two examples must suffice. In one, a resident behaves badly towards other residents. This could take many forms, the style of which may vary with different ages of residents or style of homes: one resident destroys something another cherishes; a group bullies or undermines someone; an individual persistently annoys other residents, in a real sense interfering in their lives. The second example is when a resident leaves the home without agreement of staff.

Another type of tension occurs when a member of staff sees actions by another which are judged to be harmful to the well-being of a resident.

A simplified picture of working in an ethical way would be to imagine that the worker would refer to a set of values and the solution would emerge. That is rarely the case. It is probable that staff will have to struggle to work out what to do. I shall pursue the example of a resident who leaves the home without agreement. Each situation varies and demands an individualized response but there may be some general points to consider.

The starting point is to think about the nature of the responsibility of the residential home towards the resident. A home must function in accord with declarations made to the registration authority as to objectives, procedures and staffing levels and in accordance with the law. In residential child care there are detailed notes of guidance which have statutory backing. There is no equivalent in relation to residential care of adults although there is a general duty of care. So the question must be put as to whether there is authority to hold a person against their will. Since there are very few occasions when that is the case, staff are likely to be in the more complex situation where they have to work out what is ethical as well as what is legal practice.

One approach is to try to understand the behaviour. I have heard of one staff member who noticed that a resident kept walking across a busy road to try to get to some parked cars. It emerged in conversation that the resident had enjoyed going out with her husband in their car. The staff member left her own car unlocked in the yard and the resident went and sat in it, the result of good observation, listening and planning.

Second, it is useful to clarify the nature of the problem in the behaviour. Precision in the use of words and therefore checking their meaning with others is vital. Cain (1998) argues for the use of philosophy as a form of critical enquiry 'to get clear about the meaning and application of particular concepts'.

This may involve considering the language through which they are expressed, what must be the case if they (concepts) are to... apply and their logical relationships with other associated concepts. What for example is it 'to know'? How is this distinct from 'believing'? Is 'intuition' a form of 'knowing'? Again, how do you tell a therapeutic relationship when you see one? (Cain, 1998, p. 122)

In terms of a person leaving a home, it would be possible to specify how different people perceive the behaviour. In particular, this could be followed with whether the actions are thought to constitute a risk. Some young people and adults might be thought to be vulnerable to assault. Others may be thought to be taking decisions which may involve an element of risk but are of the order of risk which others in society are allowed to take. Third, some people might be judged not to be wholly competent to determine what they should do.

This last group raises particular dilemmas for staff. In a passage quoted earlier, Stevenson (1996, p. 212) states staff need 'to recognize an equivalent moral duty to protect a vulnerable person'. Relatives, others in society and residents all probably expect the same. The question moves from *whether* staff should intervene to *how* they are to intervene given this duty to protect. As mentioned earlier, current law on mental competence allows little action outside the formality of Mental Health Acts and the National Assistance Act 1948. Staff are left with a duty to protect and an expectation from different groups of people that they will do so.

One way to proceed, recognizing the complexity of the decisions, is to share the dilemmas with interested parties, in particular residents, prospective residents, staff, management, relatives, registration authority and police. From such discussions policy and practice can be devised and written down. An imaginary example follows:

In Meadowlands Residential Home for older adults we want people to be able to exercise their full rights as citizens but also want to provide appropriate services to support. We recognize a responsibility to provide care when necessary.

Meadowlands is the residents' home. Residents may go out or leave when they wish. It is helpful if staff are informed when residents are going out, in particular in case there is a fire, but we know that this will not always happen. There are times when there may be different views as to whether residents should go out, frequently because they are thought to be at some risk. We are not allowed to lock doors in such a way as would prevent residents from leaving. Therefore, there is no way in which we can, or should, forcibly prevent someone from going out.

However, we are aware of our responsibilities as staff and of the anxiety of relatives and residents. Where people are concerned we would like to discuss the nature of the concern and to consider what action might be taken. It may be appropriate to produce a written plan which sets out what should be done.

In terms of a document like this, thought has to be given to what is to be written down. Staff have to consider values and potential tensions between them. They will then need to consider what degree of oversight and intervention is proper.

Focusing on people's rights, they may judge that the resident, as an adult, has made a decision; whether or not that decision conflicts with what staff or others think best, nobody has a right nor a duty to stop the person from leaving. Nevertheless, staff may think it proper to discuss their concerns with the resident, as they might with anyone else for whom they had concerns.

It is more complex if the resident is thought not always competent to make the decision. One possibility is to talk with people when they are thought more competent as to what should happen when they seem less able to care for themselves. Oversight is another technique to consider: for example, to walk with the resident. This may be extended to forms of intervention which endeavour to persuade the person to change their course of action, perhaps to return to their sitting room.

Boundary management is a form of manipulating the environment for a desired end. For example, the route from the front door to the road might be made less obvious, by constructing a hedge or wall which naturally leads to a walk around the home, rather than to the road.

It is essential that discussions are held as to the actions which are morally good. Staff face complex decisions and need as much authority as possible, rather than the common approach of ignoring the problem and leaving the staff to manage impossible tensions. Particular approaches, for example the electronic tagging of residents, will raise specific dilemmas which have to be thought through. Decisions have to be made in the light of theoretical frameworks, beliefs and values. Are we promoting the value and dignity of this person? Are we caring for them?

A different sort of tension for staff arises when there are conflicts of interest between two workers, or between worker and agency. Workers have loyalties to colleagues: these are people they know and with whom they work. In addition people learn from childhood not to 'tell tales' on others. Increasingly, staff are likely to be aware of the serious impact on someone's career of questioning their work. The starting point should be the creation of an environment in which people expect to learn and to talk to each other about their work. Workers should not let bad practice go without comment: it becomes harder to say something on a later occasion. So the aim should be to talk to the other worker: 'I was surprised that you…' 'I wonder why you…' Approaches like this can lead to discussion about alternative ways of handling difficult situations.

In short discussions like this it is hard not to be dogmatic. So it is easy to write that staff must confront bad practice. Putting that into effect requires judgement: how bad is what I saw? how typical is it of this person's work? is their approach different from mine but as good, or is it, at least, acceptable? Any of these decisions are harder in an environment which does not encourage openness. In the extreme, a worker has a responsibility to report to managers the actions of a colleague if they believe them to be harmful to a resident. Some codes of practice now write in an obligation of this type.

Conflict between resident and agency interests raises different dilemmas. The worker is employed by the agency and takes on to work as a responsible member of the organization. Various scenarios can be examined. One that is common in residential homes is how staff are to help residents represent their collective interest if that is in conflict with the aims of the organization. This might happen when an organization plans to change or close residential homes. Burton (1989) writes of residents as well as staff lobbying councillors when plans were put forward to close their home. The manager of the home was 'upbraided by the Director of Social Services who could not accept that older people, users of the services he managed, had not been manipulated into attending the meeting or that they had genuine objections to the plan being put forward' (p. 61). In this example the position is more complicated because the staff do have an interest in change; they have to be able to tease out how they are to support residents, assert their own views and behave properly as employees.

Another type of issue arises when staff do not think that there are adequate resources properly to provide for residents. Sometimes this takes the form of: 'This resident should move to somewhere more suitable.' Once again there is need to search at motivation: there are the interests of other residents who may be affected adversely by a resident; there are interests of staff who may find the care and management of this person difficult; there are the interests of the resident, who may not be cared for adequately. There can be no rules of thumb. Staff members have to examine both the nature of their concerns and the options available, if possible with colleagues, if appropriate with individual residents,

A third potential conflict of interest arises when a staff member believes that a resident is being harmed and the management does not accept this or makes insufficient response. Anyone who reads numerous enquiry reports into scandals will know the frequency with which it is revealed that someone had raised the concerns earlier. Sometimes the person who made the complaint is new to the home, a student or new member of staff. The knowledge that a new pair of eyes can see malpractice which others no longer notice should serve as encouragement to new members of staff to express their doubts. If a worker judges the response to a complaint to be insufficient there are several avenues open: to raise the matter with the registration authority; to seek the help of outside bodies which aim to support workers who 'blow the whistle'; or to seek advice from an association such as the Social Care Association or, in the future, the General Social Care Council in England (and the related bodies in other parts of the UK, still to be given titles when this was written).

The creation of a culture in which workers and residents take an active stance in questioning and debating what goes on, is likely to expose malpractice and, more generally, to counter discrimination.

The task in thinking about an ethical base is to clarify our own ideas and those of others. What are taken to be facts may turn out to be values; facts which do not fit with our own framework may be discarded. The certainty that the sun orbited the earth led to the discarding of evidence that did not fit the framework. The assumption that the natural relationship of parent to child created a taboo or barrier that would prevent sexual abuse, resulted in the abuse of children being denied. So we need critical enquiry. But we also need to use that enquiry to construct a framework for practice which links beliefs, theory and values.

Beliefs and values are at the heart of good residential practice. Lists of such values may have some use in promoting thought. But they have a parallel danger that they may be used without analysis to justify any action. We know the potential fallibility of the argument that people are doing something for the good of another. In residential work staff too often have thought they knew what was in someone else's interest.

Residential work will not be successful unless staff believe in the value of what they are doing; if they are to value others, they must maintain their own self-esteem; to do that, in turn they must be valued.

7

Researching Residential Life

Introduction

I have claimed in different parts of this book that one of the keys to successful practice is a search to understand the experience of residents. I have no doubt that putting energy into trying to understand is important in its own right. However, the search should not be solely an individual experience in which one person tries to understand another. The search should also draw on others, most obviously the individuals themselves and their relatives, but also people who have views which may be of help in understanding.

Sometimes ideas are presented in the form of a theory. The fact that something is called a *theory* does not make it true, as I have argued in earlier chapters. One of the ways in which ideas and theories may be tested is through research which is a form of enquiry. In this chapter I look at the value of research and at its limitations. I hope that this has relevance for students undertaking research projects, but also for residents and staff inside the home so that they can consider, first, whether or not they want to undertake research themselves and, second, whether they want to give permission to others to do research work in their home.

Differing approaches to knowledge

There are many different types of writing on residential work. A book may present one person's story of their life or work: the material is autobiographical. Another may be a text like this one which aims to distil and present current thinking on practice. Reports into homes, whether as part of regular inspections or special enquiries, are a third category. A fourth type of information is that which comes from studies presenting research findings.

In examining the literature with its numerous claims, for example as to what constitutes good practice, attention must be given to the nature of the evidence: on what basis is this writer making a statement? In addition, it is essential to consider the quality of the material. Some research is weak, other strong; the account of one person may contain better analysis than another; ideas may be expressed more or less cogently.

One of the key tests of any study is whether it makes sense to the people who live and work in residential homes. This is not to propose that people should dispense with any material which does not match their own stance, a highly dangerous position. Rather, it is to argue that ideas have to be examined and tested by the reader.

So the fact that a work is termed 'research', 'autobiography' or 'textbook' does not mean that one is more reliable than another; each views what is happening in different ways. However, the way in which evidence is collected and examined does differ, and clarity about the difference is essential.

Let us take an example of the way someone might describe an event, whether talking, recording in a log or writing in a book.

A resident, Susan, walks into a sitting room. Immediately, and without consulting anyone else in the room, she turns the TV to another channel. A staff member shouts at her, 'You're always doing that.'

What validity should be attached to the statement? Presuming that the person reporting the event is endeavouring to record accurately, we are still faced with the need to interpret. First, we can consider the meaning. What is meant by 'shouting'? Is this the typical loud speech of that staff member or is it unusual? Is there any indication as to whether shouting is thought to be acceptable. Second, we need to know something of the context: the type of residential home; the ways in which decisions are made; the role of staff. Indeed, it is possible that the other residents in the room have agreed that Susan can watch this programme and that the staff member does not know this.

A research study would examine questions like these more broadly in a particular home or in several homes. In this example the focus of a study would be to try to understand aspects of shouting: perhaps, frequency, interactions between individual staff members and individual residents, the experiences of staff members and residents, types of occasions when shouting is more frequent or the acceptability of shouting.

Research should aim to provide disciplined enquiry into a topic. For example, the assumptions that people have about shouting could be compared to reality: frequency, degree of concern or explanation. Good research should provide evidence; ideas and hypotheses should be examined. This has particular importance in attempting to understand people because there are so many assumptions as to people's behaviour.

I have heard staff talk about some older people as being 'happily confused'. The idea is that the people are confused in orientation but that they are not distressed by this. Imagine an older person who sets off to look for a long dead spouse and is redirected by a staff member; she/he sits down and smiles. I am suspicious of assumptions that the person is happy. I have met older people who talk with anxiety about something being wrong in parts of their brain. Staff have far more experience of working with confused older people than I; their view may be based on what could be termed 'practice wisdom'. But are they right? A research project could be established to examine the experience of confusion.

The role of research in examining the assumptions on which practice is based is vital. Atherton (1989, p. 101) argues that practice depends on assumptions of staff about how things are done in a particular home. Such assumptions, or myths, may be reinforced by anecdotes. Relying on such practice myths is as dangerous as relying on individual feelings. Research is one way of moving towards testing assumptions.

These examples pose questions as to the basis of the understanding on which practice is based. How do people come to an understanding of an event and an explanation for it?

Research into practice

Distinctions are often made between research and other forms of enquiry. Thus, staff within a home could collect information to review practice but this is different from the research enquiry of an outsider. Outside researchers have a degree of distance from life in the home but are not necessarily impartial: they may have very strong views. Importantly also, more attention is being given to partnership in research between external research workers and insiders.

Imagine that in some way 'shouting' has been established as the focus of a research study. At this stage researchers often want to rush into action to find out what is going on. However, it is necessary to pause for reflection because without understanding more of the background to the enquiry, it will not be possible to focus the research. One of the major weaknesses of student research projects is that they pursue a topic, such as shouting, without defining what they want to know. If this happens, the research will get out of control. I am using the term 'researcher' to mean a person who, probably with others, intends to carry out research, not someone necessarily who is external to the establishment and trained in research methods.

Some background work primarily is reflective:

- *What is the nature of the interest in the topic?* Is it from certain groups? Does the researcher have a personal interest or personal knowledge? For example, what has been the researcher's experience of shouting at others, being shouted at or seeing other people shout? How powerful have these been? Are there any anecdotes which illustrate concern or different perspectives?

- *How did the research get set up?* Who is commissioning it, that is asking for it to take place and funding it? Do they have ideas of how they wish to use the information?

- *Accountability.* What limits, if any, are put on control by the researchers of the activity? What will happen if the findings run counter to the views of others, whether those commissioning the research, the residents or the staff? Indeed, researchers have to consider what is the potential impact of publicizing research findings. Alternatively, how will action be taken if the work of the researchers is thought too intrusive into the lives of residents?

- *Ethics.* Researchers have direct influence in the way the project is managed, the findings are interpreted and written. What is to be the role of those who are the subjects of the research study? How will the material be checked against their understandings? What about confidentiality and power?

- *Importance* is a further aspect for reflection: is the proposed topic worth the energy and the disturbance?

- *Directed enquiry* is a term to describe the effort that has gone into defining the area for study, recognizing its strengths and limitations. Research should not be like a scatter-gun that is fired off in the hope that some shot will hit a target.

The reflection should lead to defining the precise focus of the enquiry. There is nothing wrong with an enquiry being exploratory if that is its purpose, for example, to find out whether residents or staff are concerned about shouting. Alternatively, a focus could be narrower, perhaps trying to chart the frequency and causation of shouting.

Alongside this reflection is an examination of work already undertaken on this or a related topic. It may be that there is earlier research on shouting in a particular type of residential home or on shouting in a related field of work with people, perhaps nursing or teaching. How did those researchers carry out their study? What methods appeared to be successful? What did they find out? Do we want to replicate any of those methods for comparative purposes?

Next comes the planning of the research. This is the move from focus to method. Consideration has to be given at this stage as well as earlier to ethics: the research is not to be abusive nor run counter to the well-being of residents; people must give informed consent to participation; the power relationship of researcher to residents and staff must be examined, as must what is meant by confidentiality and the use to which the findings may be put.

Taking account of the focus of the enquiry and the consideration of ethics, methods have to be worked out. There are numerous ways to collect information: observation, questionnaires, interviews, asking people to write about their experiences or keep a diary, collecting statistics. Skills are required in any of these, for example in producing the sorts of questions which will encourage people to respond and will get at relevant information. Ways of recording information have to be determined. The scope of the project must allow for completion with the available resources.

The plan for the research is negotiated with the insiders and put into effect. Information is collected and recorded. Some people consider that the findings of research follow automatically from the collection of the data. In part this may be right: a table could be produced that charts the numbers of shouting episodes, the occasions on which they took place, the time of day, and the people involved. However, research workers have to find ways to write up their observations. This is not just a neutral, supposedly scientific process: necessarily, it involves selection and ordering of material and consideration of how it is to be presented. The researcher must be true to the material collected but, at best, has skills in describing and in analysing what has been found. Thus, the research report might show the sorts of shouting events about which people were most concerned and explanations for their occurrence.

Such findings and analysis should be considered by insiders as to the extent to which they help understanding of their experience.

Information like this would allow consideration by all stakeholders of whether or not to take specific action following the conclusion of the research. Research reports frequently end with a list of recommendations. In the main these are unhelpful because it is for the organization, not the researcher, to determine what to do. The core job of the researcher is to present findings, even if they are unwelcome to the insiders. What happens has to be worked out from the inside. Of course there may be occasions when the ideas of researchers as to what might be done are wanted and of use to the organization. Nevertheless, the general message to researchers should be to avoid lists of recommendations.

Social research in residential homes

Gilbert (1992, p. xi) states that 'Social research has to be concerned with understanding, not just description.' It looks at *what* is happening, *how* it is happening and *why* it is happening.

In this brief description it becomes apparent that research is an attempt to study. Such study raises questions as to the nature of evidence, knowledge and truth. There are major debates in research writing as to the nature of truth: are some methods of collecting data more reliable than others? At its most simple, one group has been described as *positivists*, in that they seek information which has scientific validity: given x and y, z will always follow. Others argue that people's experiences are not like that and to search for a presumed scientific objectivity distorts what happens. To understand people, they would contend, you must take account of their perceptions of what has happened.

Smith (1998) exposes the limitations, indeed the distortions, introduced by those who demand evidence-based practice, in the sense of certainty of input and outcome. He sets social science research in the context of human experience 'because the social world is ineradicably unpredictable'. The context of events changes with time and space. His list of advice includes the following paraphrased from Braithwaite (1993):

> Don't expect anything always to work on its own. Prefer integrated strategies that are dynamically responsive to environmental change to static approaches based on a single type of theory.

Although the tasks of researcher and residential worker are different, there are parallels with the search of residential staff first to understand residents' experience and behaviour and, second, to think about the consequences for their work. This is shown, for example, in

- trying to understand the resident's reality;
- recognizing difference as well as similarity between residents' experiences and even between an individual resident's behaviour on different occasions;
- repeatedly testing whether theoretical explanations are helpful in understanding what is happening and what to do;
- specifically, not using theory as a blunderbuss to force events into a predetermined order.

Other characteristics of good research should also be part of good residential practice: checking information, precision in the use of language, questioning assumptions which are taken for granted.

Research is not truth: it aims to describe and explain, but remains an interpretation of material by the researcher. Researchers differ not only in methods but in their skills. Some are better able than others to get people to talk about their work or to see significant clues through their observation.

Given different views as to the nature of reality, it is not surprising that there are different research methods One distinction is between *qualitative* and *quantitative* methods. Quantitative research is that in which information is collected in such a way that it can be translated into statistical data. The term 'qualitative research' is used to refer to methods in which people examine the quality of an experience; qualitative researchers do not claim that other methods have not got quality, in the sense of high standards. Today many researchers will combine statistical and qualitative methods.

In qualitative research, attempts are made to understand process and experience: the meaning of events to the people involved. In addition, taken for granted assumptions can be questioned. Such research methods are valuable in trying to understand and explain what happens in residential work. Qualitative research methods should be adopted because they are regarded as appropriate to the task, not because the researcher is fearful of statistics nor because the researcher thinks the technique does not have to be rigorous. In any method, it is essential that the researcher is rigorous, persistent, open to new information and able to account for the collection of data.

Comments from Morse (1994) illustrate some of these points:

> The process of doing qualitative research represents a challenge because procedures for organizing our images are ill defined and rely on a process of *inference, insight, logic and luck,* and, eventually, *with creativity and hard work,* the results emerge as a coherent whole. The laboratory of the qualitative researcher is everyday life. (p. 1)

Qualitative research, he claims, should aim at:

1. flexibility in the research process;
2. placing social life in a natural context;
3. being concerned with process as well as outcome;
4. explanations that are adequate at the level of meaning, although caution is needed in attempting to ascribe causation (summarized from pp. 158ff).

Such research, he continues, has the potential to:

1. reflect the subjective reality of those people who are the focus of the research;
2. continue over time;
3. involve subjects in collaborative research;
4. provide clear theoretical frameworks for empirical work (summarized from pp. 158ff).

Research should also be conducted to high ethical standards. We know that, in rare situations, that has not always been the case in that some researchers have falsified their data. However there are ethical considerations in much of the day-to-day activity of research. At the heart of many tensions is the relationship between researcher and researchee, the person being studied. And at the heart of this relationship is power.

The researcher has considerable power in setting the agenda for the research, defining the methods and interpreting the results. Various writers examine the morality of researching others' lives and ways in which the subjects of the research may gain power in relation to the study. Tozer and Thornton (1995) and Peace (1998) describe projects in which older people were used as research advisers so that their perspective was included in planning and implementation.

There are also debates as to what researchers should reveal about what they find. In whose interests is it to report? How is the researcher to take account of different interests in the way the statements about findings are worded? What responsibility does the researcher have for the use others may make of the findings?

So staff working in residential homes, faced with a request for research in their home, should be considering with residents whether or not they wish the research to take place. What influence do they want to have on the process or the reporting? In whose interests is the research? The detail is important as is the recognition of differing interests of researcher and researchee. The starting point for researchers should be ensuring that they have authority to report on what they find: they need to avoid the type of gagging clause which will allow publication of the research only if the findings suit the commissioner of the research. However, the organization that manages the residential home, the staff or the people who live in the home all have other interests: perhaps for privacy, respect, ensuring, as they see it, the accuracy of the report.

Pursuing the implications of some of these seemingly straightforward points highlights the tension. A not infrequent scenario is that of the researcher taking one view of an event and wanting to use certain phrases to describe it. Any of the insiders may take an alternative view either of what happened or of the explanation for it. Each group asserts that it wants accurate description of the event but the accounts are different. I highlight the potential tension to illustrate dilemmas and the sort of negotiation which needs to take place.

Many researchers will try to ensure the accuracy of their findings by producing preliminary findings which are checked by the researchees. Others may state that they will not use any information arising from the collection of data unless the participants are happy with the way the material is used. Another approach, which I have adopted in some projects, is to accept any rewording of a report which is requested provided that, in the perception of the researcher, it does not distort the findings; the researcher retains the right to use the words he/she chooses but to allow the research subjects space to put an alternative position if they disagree with statements made. Yet another approach is to suggest that research should arise from research subjects rather than the researchers. An example of this is Miller and Gwynne's 1972 study of homes for people with physical disabilities.

> It was a group of residents at Le Court who first persuaded us of the need for research into residential care for the severely disabled; and in the course of the project we collaborated with the Management committee, staff and residents in

designing and implementing certain changes in the running of the home. This experience was invaluable in forcing us to clarify our ideas and allow us to begin to test them in a real life setting. (p. xi)

The researchers (pp. 16–38) describe the process of the approach made to them by residents; their assumption that the letter had come from a member of staff; their 'shock and guilt' when they realized their mistake; and the pull and counter-pull on them as to whether or not to take on this project.

From this source we were subjected to an unrelenting pressure, overt and covert, to get us to undertake practical research. That we were ambivalent about this demand is shown by the contrast between our expressions of concern and our slowness to act. (p. 19)

Their study is a useful example also of research writing which is both personal and rigorous. As I have argued elsewhere:

I draw on personal experience of myself and others as well as on larger research studies. Thus I aim to combine the personal and the political, believing that the best of social work research and practice recognizes the significance of one's own experiences, the impact on oneself of others' experiences and, at the core, the meaning of events for those live through them. (Clough, 1996a, p. 4)

In examining research findings it is useful to be aware of the researcher's stance as well as method. Is the researcher an insider or an outsider? Does the researcher participate in any way in the life of the home? Has the researcher a prior position which is being tested?

Research findings may be interpreted and used incorrectly. Miller and Gwynne's (1972) study illustrates the way in which the ideas of the researchers may be taken out of context and distorted by later commentators. The most important of these distortions relates to their models of homes.

As mentioned in Chapter 4, they outlined three models of residential practice: warehousing, horticultural and organizational. The horticultural model, with its emphasis on development, has immediate attractions. Yet the authors reject this, arguing for the organizational model which caters for both dependence and independence.

Frequently, I have heard people use Miller and Gwynne's work to promote a developmental or horticultural model, seemingly not aware that the authors explicitly recognized the limitations of this. I suspect that the reason why their message has been distorted is that they had powerful and emotive words to describe two of their models, but not the third. The example shows that even with what I consider to be very good research, it is important for all parties to check what was said and whether they think its methods and conclusions to be valid. Given that much research will not be of this quality, it is even more important to ensure that people have the knowledge and confidence critically to examine findings.

Research is not truth although it is an attempt to look at what happens in a way that differs from an individual impression. Research, as Hardiker (1989) states, is 'An intellectual journey in which researchers must constantly engage with their purposes, subject theories, methods and data'.

8

Managing in a Residential Home

What sort of management?

When life is complicated and demanding in residential homes it is easy to blame others, and managers, internal and external, are an easy prey. The arguments will be only too familiar. If only they would:

- give us enough staff;
- stop all the form filling;
- decide what we are meant to be doing;
- stand up to the silly expectations of inspectors or relatives or anyone;
- take control of what is going on;
- take responsibility for what is going on;
- be around when life is difficult;
- and so on.

There is widespread recognition in writing on residential work of the importance of leadership. The focus, drive, commitment, style and competence of the leader make an immense difference to the quality of care. There is much less written on the sorts of organizational structures within the home and outside which support or impede good practice. How accurate is it when staff or residents blame internal and external managers? Is it fair to hold managers responsible for not providing the conditions for effective practice?

Approaches to understanding management often develop from one of two very different starting points. The first is to see management as an everyday activity of which everyone has experience: management of a residential home is doing on a larger scale what we all do in managing other aspects of our lives, in particular managing households – the combination of buildings, finance and lifestyle in the places where we live. The other starting point is to see management as a highly complex activity, one which may be technical and scientific, and demands special knowledge and skills. Both have elements of truth.

I start with what we know from our own experiences of managing our lives and indeed our work environments. In managing our households we need:

- to have or create enough resources;
- to deal with the present demands (servicing of the boiler, mending the washing machine, getting the food in);
- to deal with the present in the context of the future: is it worth getting the washing machine repaired? what life is there in the machine? have we the resources for a new one? what other commitments have we got or do we plan?
- to plan our time;
- to negotiate with other household members about arrangements for living, including who will do what;
- to develop systems for tasks, whether the payment of bills, the filing of documents or the cleaning of the house.

The list could be continued to take account, for example, of negotiations with neighbours or considering what to do when external changes occur over which one has no control, perhaps losing a job or a major development around one's house changing the character of the place and the reason why it was purchased.

Yet it is dangerous not to recognize that the task of management of a residential home differs from that of household management. Regulation authorities are right to demand expertise by qualification or experience, although they may not be sure of what comprises either. People who have set up residential homes sometimes come unstuck because they cannot manage well enough the complexity and interrelatedness of the tasks of managing the home. And it is well recognized that people who are good at doing the work do not necessarily make good managers. Management demands knowledge and skills.

However, recognizing the importance of these very skills and knowledge can lead managers themselves or theorists on management to focus on the technical and to neglect the ordinary. Management is about creating the conditions in which people can do everyday things.

The person who manages the home may be known by various titles: manager, officer in charge, warden, director or head. The task is that of holding the prime responsibility for the functioning of the home, including the boundary between the home and the external world. The manager may also be the owner. If that is not the case, there will be external managers and/or a management committee. (For convenience I shall use the word 'manager' on its own in this chapter to refer to the manager within the home, and always add 'external' or 'outside' when I refer to a manager who is based outside the home.)

Management is often portrayed as if the task and the skills needed can be neatly defined. The Residential Forum (1997, p. 3) recognizes that there 'is no agreed definition of management nor of a manager'; management is seen as art and as science; some consider managers to have skills that can be applied in any setting while others argue that managers must know their product. The report states that there has been 'little research and analysis of what the management of a Home or of a residential service actually includes' (p. 3).

The Residential Forum continues its own analysis, seeing management as a continuous process of:

planning and organizing;

managing in practice (doing or implementing);

co-ordinating;

monitoring;

reviewing and evaluating;

changing and improving. (1997, p. 3)

Burton (1998) places the management of a home within the context of the management of an organization. 'Therefore, for good residential care to become an established reality, both "inside" and "outside" management must in fact work together towards one goal – meeting residents' needs' (p. xv). Later he writes: 'As a process, management is the organization required to get the job done.' He notes that while 'The structure of such management has the person doing the job at its centre', it is essential 'to include as part of management all those people and resources that surround, support, co-ordinate and monitor the work of the central figure' (pp. 45–6).

He contends that in the last 30 years, mistakenly, 'pretentious and superior notions... have split management from doing' (p. 46).

The effective organization for residential care is one which not only *allows* the staff to work in ways which meet the agreed needs and wants of residents; the effective organization will *support* staff in their determination to work well for residents. The test of management is whether it makes it easier or harder for the staff to do their work.

Organizational theory

The tasks of residential homes vary significantly from place to place. However, in any home the management has to ensure the delivery of the primary task, that is the function for which the unit exists. It is this ability to know what is the core activity and to provide for its creation and survival that is the central management task. How do differing understandings of the working of organizations impact on this task?

Any reader of this book will have experiences of many different organizations: schools, universities, hospitals, social services departments, residential homes, voluntary organizations, trusts, private companies, local and central government departments. Whether as worker or service user, the contacts with some will have been good, while those with others have been awful. The temptation is to put the differences down to the individual people with whom one has contact and, indeed, this may be a part of the explanation. Another temptation is to ascribe responsibility to common, stereotypical assumptions that all publicly managed residential homes are like this, and all privately managed homes are like that.

However, the structure of the individual organization has an immense impact on what happens: on the staff who work there; the values that are held important; the systems for selection of staff; the mechanisms for decision making; the way in which performance is evaluated; the definition of task; and the characteristics of the organization.

While we want the services that welfare organizations produce, what Burton calls 'the doing', we may not like the organization in which the activity takes place. We want the nursing in a hospital or the support services in a residential home but we may not like the organizations that run them. Hasenfeld (1992) summarizes the ambivalence that exists towards welfare organizations: they are 'expected to embody the values of caring and commitment, trust and responsiveness to human need' but they also represent formidable bureaucracies, burdened by incomprehensible rules:

> Despite the ubiquity of human service organizations in the lives of people, and their primary role in influencing our welfare and well-being, they remain an enigma. To the general public these organizations, be they schools, hospitals,

mental health centres, or welfare departments, are viewed as symbols of the caring society, a manifestation of the societal obligation to the welfare and well-being of its citizens. But they are also viewed as wasteful, fostering dependency, obtrusive and controlling. (p. 3)

Most writers consider Taylor, writing in the 1900s, to be the founder of organizational theory. The core of his approach was that organizations can be understood by the application of scientific method. Pollitt (1993) states that Taylor concluded that the fundamental weakness in organizations was loss through inefficiency and that the remedy lay in systematic management: the best management, he claimed, was a true science. In this approach the organization is seen as a machine: its failings can be understood and remedied; the consistent application of scientific principles will lead to improved performance.

A variant on this model, Hasenfeld suggests, is the *rational–legal model*. This has an organization in which there is a rational division of tasks and a formal decision-making structure. It is accompanied by a legal allocation to positions: the consequent distribution of authority, together with the rights and duties of each position are based on impersonal rules, universally applied. Hasenfeld's main criticism of the analysis is that it ignores informal structures.

A very different model is the *human relations approach*. Hasenfeld states that this approach recognizes that 'the job requirements and conditions of work have profound psychological consequences for staff'. In the human services (that is those in which the core activity is people working with other people for their welfare) 'it is assumed that the attitudes of the staff to their work situation and their co-workers will have direct consequences to how they relate to their own clients' (p. 27). The emphasis on 'the psychological needs of the workers' and 'democratic participation as determinants of organizational effectiveness', Hasenfeld suggests, risks ignoring strong environmental factors, for example the volume of paperwork, low wages or poor working conditions (p. 28).

He prefers an *institution–environmental* model in which the key to understanding organizations is to be found in the interactions that occur between organizations and their environments. Indeed, the interplay of political and institutional forces may be the essential determinants of how service organizations define and implement their functions.

How far do any of these descriptions of organizations reflect life and work in a residential home? Do they help to form a view of the type of an organization which will produce the best residential care?

Producing the goods and services

Patti (1992), in an introduction to Hasenfeld's work, argues that one of the distinctive characteristics of human services agencies is 'their reliance on both professional workers and consumers to co-produce outcomes' (p. viii). Thus, a residential home differs from many other organizational systems in that the outcomes are dependent on residents as well as staff. This means that we have to consider both the conditions which allow staff to work most effectively and the conditions which allow residents to live most fully. Of course, there may be common factors.

Another way of looking at systems in residential homes has been to compare a factory process with that in a residential home. This may seem an inappropriate analogy but has been used by the Tavistock Institute to advantage in understanding process. Thus, Miller and Gwynne (1972) look at the process of converting raw materials in a factory into a product. They contend that to see residents in this way as people to whom things are done has been a part of regimented residential care. Their preferred model sees residents in effect as both product and resource: the system exists to provide resources for residents but residents are themselves a part of the equation on the resources side.

Later variations of the process model have distinguished between *output* and *outcome*. Output is taken to be what is produced, for example a meal cooked. Outcome is what the meal is like, the quality both of the product and the experience. The Residential Forum (1996) defines various terms as follows:

INPUTS = What is put in to provide a service

PROCESS = The practice of providing the service

OUTPUTS = The service delivered

OUTCOMES = The effect of the service provided. (p. 18)

The process is the activity that transforms the input.

Some writers see outcome as the view of the resident on the product. The resident's perception of the product is a central part of the outcome but should not be taken to be the only view. A meal may be well cooked and served in an environment which is thought to be satisfactory; yet a resident, depressed or unhappy for reasons other than the food, may not enjoy the meal. Analyses can distort in other ways in that aspects are presented as discrete when they may be intertwined: in some services the 'product' is a combination of process and output, for example, when a person is being bathed.

There are many key determinants of good residential practice other than organizational structure, of which resources is one of the most important. Yet if we recognize that organization and management cannot on their own make for successful practice, we must recognize also that successful residential practice is dependent on sound organizational structure and process. An understanding of what happens in organizations and of the effects of different approaches should improve the quality of residential work.

However, the danger still exists of seeing both organizational and management theory as a science, as if there is a correct formula which can be correctly applied.

Morgan's (1986) use of metaphors to understand organizations is a helpful way of escape from a notion of scientific certainty. 'Effective managers and professionals in all walks of life', he contends, 'have to become skilled in the art of "reading" the situations that they are attempting to organize and manage' (p. 11). 'Organizations are many things at once' (p. 339):

> In trying to understand an organizational situation we have to be able to cope with these different and potentially paradoxical meanings, identifying them through some form of decomposition while retaining a sense of their interrelationship and essential integration. (p. 342)

His own metaphors to understand organizations are numerous. Organizations can be seen as:

- *Machines* with 'interlocking parts that each play a clearly defined role in the function of the whole'.
- *Organisms*, a metaphor, which 'focuses attention on understanding and managing organizational "needs" and environmental relations'. There are different types of 'organism' suited to different purposes.
- *Brains*: attention is given 'to the importance of information processing, learning and intelligence'.
- *Cultures*: 'Organization is now seen to reside in the ideas, values, norms, rituals, and beliefs that sustain organizations as social constructed realities'.
- *Systems of government* highlighting 'the different sets of interests, conflicts, and power plays that shape organizational activities'.

- *Psychic prisons* 'where people become trapped by their own thoughts, ideas, and beliefs, or by preoccupations originating in the unconscious mind'.
- *Instruments of domination* where the emphasis is placed on the 'potentially exploitative aspects of organization'.

The core purpose

Whether in households or in organizations it is frequent for certain mundane events to be noticed but not acted on: a light bulb needs to be changed, the toilet roll has been finished, or there are marks to be wiped off walls. One reason for the inaction is that the tasks may not be assigned to anyone. A solution adopted in some organizations is to place responsibility on individuals in ever smaller detail for any event that occurs. In residential work (as, I believe, in households) this is mistaken for it denies the involvement of everybody in the responsibility for the life of the organization: too much demarcation is unhelpful.

Yet managers are likely to recognize the fact that frequently it is they who notice things that need doing and they who act on them. So it should be. The responsibility of the manager is to keep an eye on what is happening, to be aware of the way the detail affects daily life and to do something about it. That is not to argue that the manager should not delegate by asking others to do things, nor that others should not put in a new light bulb. It is to recognize that a part of the job of the manager is to do things.

How is this active, 'light bulb changing' manager in a residential home to sort out priorities? How is a balance to be struck between the involvement in the detail and other tasks, such as maintaining the boundaries of the home?

The test is that of the maintenance and development of the primary task of the establishment. When caught up in the life of a place there is rarely a way to be certain as to what one should be doing. Many people who write books describe the difficulty of starting and maintaining their focus on the task: some tidy their desks or work rooms before beginning; others want to be involved in more vigorous physical activity, cleaning the bath or digging the garden. These may be useful ways of starting the activity of writing, whether through creating an environment which is conducive for work or through creating space to begin thinking about the task while being physically preoccupied. Yet, many of us will recognize how easily such activities can become displacements: we end up with a clean house but no writing.

The same is true with management. The manager who earns the plaudits of the staff because he or she 'is always doing things and helping us out' may be avoiding other tasks; it is probable that the manager who is always tied up in important meetings, perhaps rarely in the home, is also avoiding what should be core activities, for example being available to staff and residents.

It is not appropriate to set out precise parameters for managers and demand that they spend set amounts of time on specific parts of their work. But it is proper that managers know that the test of how they are using their time is whether they are developing the primary task, the core purpose of the organization. It is proper that residents and staff know this also, and so are able to make demands on the manager.

The characteristics of good residential management

Analogies may be helpful in describing some of the characteristics of management. For example, the manager may be seen as producer of a play: having a vision of how things should be and aware of the subtleties of the text; recognizing that others are the key performers; listening and negotiating with the actors and stage staff; allowing things to develop in ways that had not been envisaged; providing the resources for the production.

But analogies have limits. In residential care we can describe the central activity of the manager in phrases like 'the creation of an environment for the achievement of the primary task'. Analysing the components of that management task is more complicated.

It is imperative that managers have an understanding of their role and objectives but are not forced into thinking that there are only certain means of achieving the ends. Thus if we examine a management activity like listening to staff and residents, we need to recognize that there are different ways of achieving this: formal meetings; informal discussions; suggestion boxes; various types of review and feedback, and so on. Some may be more suitable to particular environments but the establishment of the procedure does not ensure that people feel free to put their views, that there is a serious debate of a topic or that a manager listens to what others say. Holding a staff and residents' meeting *may* create an opportunity for all these processes; but such a meeting may be heavily controlled and stifle comment.

In what follows I aim to list components of the management task, the sort of activities which in some way managers should undertake.

I start with my phrase above, *the creation of an environment for the achievement of the primary task*. This involves establishing a climate or culture conducive to the task, asserting the core purpose for which the place exists and providing appropriate resources. The tasks of residential homes vary significantly from place to place. However, in any home, this ability to know what is the core activity and to provide for its creation and survival is the central management task.

This aspect of management requires an understanding of the nature of the task in a residential home. Some people consider that management is a generic skill: people learn how to manage and can transfer their knowledge and skill to managing very different activities. Others will claim that, to manage well, you have to have worked in the field in which you are to manage. There is truth in both. To me, the essential is that a manager understands the experience of this sort of work: what it feels like to be a resident; the processes which take place within residential homes; what it feels like to be a staff member, exposed to the potential pain, vulnerability and disturbance of residents. There needs to be awareness of the implications for practice of strong forces such as power and powerlessness, independence and dependence, secrecy and openness.

Culture has been discussed in earlier parts of this book but one aspect is vital in residential work, a belief in the value of the work being undertaken, in its moral worth and in its importance to those who live there. I stress this aspect because in too much welfare work staff are disillusioned and cannot give of their best. There must be a sense of optimism, not the false optimism that everything will get better but optimism that the work makes a difference to people's lives.

What might be termed '*task leadership*' is the second component. Some might refer to this as 'professional leadership', but the word *professional* has overtones of exclusiveness and of particular professions. The activity to which I am referring includes both a theoretical and a practical understanding of the activity of residential work in that setting. As I have argued throughout this book, residential work is not atheoretical; it demands a framework for understanding people and practice. At the least the manager should recognize the importance of such theoretical and practical knowledge even if personal expertise is limited.

Included in task leadership is a responsibility for the development of the work. At best, the manager will contribute vision, ideas of how things might be. But at least the manager must ensure that there is opportunity for the vision to be at the core of the work, perhaps by bringing in external speakers to talk to staff and residents.

It is worth reinforcing a point made earlier: what may seem tedious activities demanded by others such as producing a mission statement or statement of purpose can be used for live debate as to what is and should be the core purpose of the organization. Involving stakeholders in the production of such statements has the potential for real searching for understanding of the primary task.

Successful task leadership requires the style already advocated: active listening, discussion, review, decisions about changes and ordering priorities for action.

Next I cite *the management of operations* because it is important and is easily neglected in more grandiose ideas. The manager has responsibility for finance, staffing, production of numerous services (for example, meals, care or cleaning), ordering of goods, maintenance of buildings, administrative returns and reports. This is the nuts and bolts of the work, the interface between external managers and suppliers and the life of the home. Sound management of this aspect of the work is critical to a successful home.

In large organizations many of these activities may have designated individuals. The general manager may be dependent on the expertise of these staff. It is worth remembering the old adage that 'Knowledge is power' and that it is dangerous for the general manager not to know enough about financial procedures, IT, catering or whatever. Financial management, for example, is too important to be left with financial managers alone. The general manager should know enough to be able to ask the right questions or set the parameters: 'What', might be asked, 'would the procedure be if we wanted to... present the case for... shift resources between... or try to carry these funds forward to next year?'

Good care does not just happen. The myth that running a residential home needs only the skills of running a household is as untrue as it is of running a hotel or school. Good care requires *the establishment of internal systems to produce the social care that is wanted in their home*. There are dangers of rigidity in systems. For example, institutional tendencies may overwhelm individualized care. Systems which are constructed as ends in themselves without relating to the task they are designed to accomplish become purposeless and, worse, counterproductive to the task.

The obverse, however, is equally significant. An understanding of the nature of social care *without good systems* will not produce good meals. Managers need management skills – of budgeting, menu planning, ordering, stock control, oversight of hygiene and cooking, together with the arrangements for serving food. Understanding and good intent are not enough.

Managers therefore need to ask themselves whether they can produce systems that will provide key elements of service provision, such as reliability, consistency, continuity and safety.

Working with others. Burton (1998) writes that a group he terms 'the policy elite' must recognize that it is the residents and staff who make the real changes in homes, and that the policy elite should focus on 'the primary task of providing the resources and the legislative framework within which the struggles of residents can be fruitful and fulfilling' (p. 220).

Residential care should not be an activity that is done by one group of people, the staff, to others. The process and the outcome are dependent on the negotiation between staff and residents. Managers need to recognize this and create a collaborative style of working.

Among the staff group, this is essential because the service is not just between one staff member and one resident. At times, other staff members will be on duty and will have to continue the provision of care; care, in this sense, is never finished, and one staff member leaves their work for others to continue. One way of understanding this is to see the home itself as the key worker. The manager has to ensure that the multitude of individual contacts between one staff member and one resident are in the framework of sufficient co-operation and sufficient agreement about task. Often, staff will work with residents in private, but this should not be in the sense of private deals. Private deals lead to a multitude of individual pieces of work, which are unsupported by others and indeed may be in conflict with them.

However, within the staff team there has to be individual recognition; staff are different and each will want both to be different and to have their distinctive contribution recognized. The same is true of residents. In residential child care there has been considerable attention given to the notion of 'fairness': fairness does not mean giving the same to each person at any one time; it involves wider notions of justice, in which people receive what is appropriate to their stage, perhaps their wants and needs. The task is to create an environment in which there may be special events between individual staff and residents while ensuring that special care is available to each resident. This differs from favouritism, in which some people are part of a clique and others are excluded.

The manager should aim to create an environment in which such 'specialness' can exist between staff and residents, but also recognize that staff themselves should be treated as individual and special.

Selection and training for staff. Many enquiries and reports have laid emphasis on the importance of good staff. Indeed, any of us by now may be more than a little suspicious of organizations which, in public statements, emphasize that staff are their greatest asset. Too often the words seem a parody of what happens.

The starting point for managers should be the selection of staff. Some reports, such as Warner (1992) in relation to residential child care, have also considered ways of ensuring that staff who might be damaging to residents are excluded. Selection of staff, discussed in Chapter 2, is one of the manager's most significant activities because the manager is dependent on staff for working with residents.

There are certain aspects which are fundamental to any appointment. One is that there should be a check on an applicant's qualifications and references: too many people have been appointed with false documentation. Certificates of any claimed qualification should be seen and the immediate past social care referee should be phoned for comment on the reference. Police checks should be undertaken for any staff for whom they are required.

When under pressure because of staff shortages there is a temptation to cut corners. There is abundant, and repeated, evidence that the minimum at any appointment, even of a part-time worker, is that references and qualifications must be checked. The grounds for this are clear: applicants may be fraudulent.

An aspect of selection that may also be given scant attention when under pressure is that of equality of opportunity. Countering discrimination and oppression faced by residents, which has been emphasized throughout this book, will be effective only if the approach pervades all aspects of the life of the establishment. In relation to staff appointment, the task is to ensure that all applicants are given equal opportunity and that reliance is not placed on existing networks and word of mouth. Applicants should receive details about the home, its function and the ways in which it works *and* they should receive a job description and person specification.

The first of these, the job description, lists the tasks or activities that are required of the post-holder. The person specification sets out the personal qualities required, including qualifications and experience, under two headings, essential and desirable. It is imperative that in the first category, characteristics specified are those without which someone would not be appointed. For example, is a particular qualification an essential factor, or is it desirable, in the sense that *usually* applicants who fit the requirements, will have a qualification? The main justification for such procedures is that of equality of opportunity: applicants should be able to distinguish between essential and desirable factors; managers should be able to justify the integrity of their selection. However, looking at the detail of specifications may lead to questioning of assumptions. A standard phrase for jobs that demand travelling is 'car driver essential'. In fact, nearly always the essential factor is that the job demands travelling to various locations. An applicant who does not drive a car should be able to apply and consider with the panel whether there are ways in which the travel requirement can be managed.

There is not space here to detail the arrangements for the management of staff. However, the core aspects will be listed:

1. since staff want managers who understand their work and appreciate them as individuals, managers must have knowledge of work practice and of individuals, together with the ability to communicate their recognition;

2. supervision is a more formal activity, in which there is periodic review of someone's work; staff who get good supervision frequently are surprised that what they had expected to be an intrusive exercise turns out to be a demonstration of their manager's interest in their work;

3. training and development are essential, and managers should be thinking about the topic in relation to the staff group as a whole, as well as for individuals.

Boundary control is another area where there are no precise guidelines for particular homes. The word 'boundary' has been used widely in literature on residential child care and is helpful because it conveys the notion of differences between territories: land that is 'ours' and land that is 'theirs'. In this sense decisions have to be taken about who is to be allowed to cross the boundary and what are to be the means of approving such crossings. Are there to be 'passport controls' and 'customs officers'? Which parts of the residential home are open to visitors and which are private without a specific invitation?

The move to allow people to visit homes at any time without restriction has been an understandable reaction to former, workhouse-style attempts to restrict visiting to short periods of time. Yet such open access has failed to tease out the nature of the ownership of the home: residents are living their lives and visits may not be convenient. In places with young people, staff will need to be involved in the negotiation about visits. The starting position should be that residents are able to decide whether or not they want to receive visitors and whether to do this in public or private space. Indeed, unrestricted access has posed significant security problems with staff unaware of who has entered a home.

The notion of boundary is also intended to convey the management task of establishing an external frontier inside which there is freedom for residents and staff to work out arrangements for living. This management responsibility has an element of protection, of dealing with those outside the home so that there is greater freedom for those within. Thus the manager (though not exclusively) works with external managers, neighbours and other agencies.

This function also includes the creation of a balance between privacy and openness. Both must be maintained. Privacy in some ways may seem the more obvious imperative: the home is the place where the residents live; as other people, they have the right to live away from public scrutiny. Further, it is essential that staff and residents are able to get on with their lives and work without feeling that they have to explain everything to outsiders.

Yet openness is also an imperative. Residential homes are not the same as private households; the reason people live in homes is that they need assistance with living; the activity is in part a welfare function, regulated by society. In some homes residents are not cared for properly or are maltreated. So, a key part of preventative activities is openness. There is no longer a reasonable case to be made for homes to be closed from public and professional interest. The question becomes one of trying to establish ways in which homes are properly open to the interest and scrutiny of outsiders while maintaining the authority of residents and staff for what happens in the home. The tendency has been to try to create openness by formal means: the establishment of complaints procedures with access to people external to the home and the nomination of people as independent visitors.

Formal procedures have their place. Yet the informal arrangements are the most important because they help to establish the climate. It is not easy to specify how these two aspects of privacy and openness are both to be pursued. Unlimited openness leaves residents open to potential assault from outsiders and destroys the intimacy of living: openness should not lead to invasion. Each home must work out its own pattern remembering that both openness and privacy are essentials.

The responsibility of boundary control is successfully managed only through negotiation with stakeholders. There may be differences between groups or individuals: some people may think that they should be able to visit whenever they want, which may not be wanted by residents; others may have strong views about how residents should live, for example whether residents should be able to go out from the home or have sexual relationships. The decisions about such matters should not be taken by outsiders, although they may have a legitimate interest in them.

Management needs to recognize an obligation to create a work culture in which anybody is free to ask questions or raise concerns about residential life. It has become only too clear that the idea of group loyalty above ethics is wrong and dangerous. To pursue the boundary analogy, my argument is that it is wrong to promote national interest above justice. The overriding loyalty for insiders (managers, staff and residents) is to the welfare of residents: group solidarity with work colleagues must take second place. Hopefully, the message about priorities will be understood also by visitors.

There has been earlier comment on the nature of residential work and the stress that is an aspect of the job. In particular research suggests that when staff do not feel that their work is valued they find themselves under greater stress (Penna *et al.*, 1995). Therefore managers have a responsibility to create a work environment that is as supportive of staff as possible. This will include supervision of their work, an activity which is designed to allow staff to discuss their work and to allow managers an oversight of practice.

Accountability. Managers are accountable for what happens within the home: that is, they can be called to account. This means, first, explaining what is happening and the reasons for taking decisions and second taking responsibility for decisions which are made. The nature and location of authority are often confused in residential homes; management should play a part in clarification.

Management matters

We all know that good management makes an immense difference to our work lives and to our practice. Typically, the assumption is that the responsibility for the activity of management rests solely with the manager. However, I argue that management should be negotiated, a process in which the person being managed can have an influence.

In a study of community care, Roger Hadley and I asked staff for their views on conditions for effective practice. We grouped their responses as follows:

Relationships with the user are: needs-led; open and honest.

Relationships with the organization encourage: discretion and autonomy; multiple accountability; continuity and security; an understanding of the organizational worlds; participation and the freedom to speak out.

Relationships with colleagues are based on: shared values; trust and integrity; collaborative working.

Relationships with the wider social and political system recognize: possibility of improvement; potential to influence.

Personal development is encouraged by: use of skills; opportunities for development. (Hadley and Clough, 1996, p. 164)

From the list I want to highlight two aspects: staff wanted to be able to work in a straightforward way with service users; and, second, they wanted to be able to speak out.

Another factor we judged to be a significant variable was the coherence/incoherence of the organization (pp. 175–6). The same would hold true in residential work. Poor residential homes are often incoherent either in their own internal systems or in their relationships with a wider organization. The incoherence is shown in:

- confusion about what the work is really about and what really matters (the primary task);
- a focus on presentation rather than actuality;
- disputes, whether open or secret, between key personnel;
- imposition of instructions, which are not popular with staff.

Not surprisingly, in an incoherent home residents do not feel that their care is at the heart of what is important in the organization. So, coherence in which the parts, the structures and the processes within the organization work co-operatively towards common objectives, is ' critical to successful work. Common objectives in a residential home can only be achieved if workers and residents, indeed citizens, are involved in the debate and the dialogue.

However, while we know something of what people want from management, there is little which suggests that people can influence their managers' practice, indeed can *manage their managers*. If we know what we want from managers and, further, what we think we are entitled to expect, we can ensure that our agenda is a part of the process of management. Indeed, it is reasonable for managers to expect that those they are managing will understand the nature of the manager's task. And managers should be able to expect the support of staff.

There are different types of negotiation between managers, staff and residents. *Consultation* is an activity in which staff or residents are asked for an opinion but it is made clear that the decision rests with the manager; for example, managers may reserve the right to submit the budget because they are not prepared to submit an unbalanced budget. *Negotiation* is the process whereby different parties endeavour to achieve an agreed solution. Finally, *shared decision making* is an activity in which a decision is the responsibility of a group of people, whatever mix of managers, staff and residents.

However, that does not mean that managers should pass their responsibility to those who do not have the authority to undertake the task.

Structures and management

Managers fear that they may not know what is going on or that staff will not work as they want when they are not present. One response is to specify in ever greater detail the nature of the work to be undertaken.

An alternative approach is to specify not the components but the end product or outcome. The focus here is not in minutiae of what has to be included, but in whether or not the desired result is achieved.

A third style is to look for certain characteristics in staff and then to leave them to interpret what they do and how they do it.

It is a mistake to adopt only one of these solutions. They are much better seen as one of Morgan's 'metaphors', as perspectives on an activity rather than as truth. Different perspectives can be taken. In taking a photograph we can select the place from where take the shot, the type of lens to give us a wide angle or close up, and whether or not some parts of the picture are to be out of focus. Management requires an understanding that there are different ways of looking at the same scene. Somehow, avoiding rigidity, avoiding distorting the task, avoiding a looseness in which there is no hold of the activity, the manager has to get the show on the road.

Good residential work requires residents and staff to share in making and taking responsibility for decisions. This does not mean that all parties have to agree with any decision, but it does mean that there has to be a general agreement as to the systems in place for making decisions, for collecting the views of interested parties and for ensuring that they have a voice in decision making.

9

Good Enough Lifestyles

Introduction

Setting out the task for managers as the creation of an environment in which the primary task can be achieved, may seem oversimple or immensely complex. In this final chapter I move to the impact of the external world on the home, giving particular attention to demands for quality and regulation.

Any of us who have been subject to inspection, will know the stress that the event creates and the feelings that inspection demands more time than is justified. The activity of regulation may take energy away from the primary task of the residential home and yet the focus of the assessment ought to be on whether the primary task is achieved. No ~~nder~~ staff often want to tell inspectors that their work would be ~~r if~~ they did not have to give attention to presenting material for ~~~isitors~~ s.

~~however~~er, the option of being left to get on with the job without ~~~al~~ eview is not a satisfactory option as there have been (and are) too many poor residential homes. So the focus of the chapter is on the tension between internal and external worlds.

Management of the environment

I start with a focus on the residential home as a place where people live: the impact of the buildings and facilities in the creation of the environment, perhaps termed 'culture', 'climate' or 'lifestyle'. The residential home as a base for living is at the boundary of internal and external worlds.

Our relationship with the place where we live has a major impact on identity. Franklin (1996, pp. 79–96) examines different ways of viewing housing: as design; economic asset; context for service delivery; institution and lived experience. In developing the last of these categories, that of the dwelling as lived experience, she quotes various themes listed by Despres (1991):

home as security and control

home as reflection of one's ideas and values

home as acting upon and modifying one's dwelling

home as permanence and continuity

home as relationship with family and friends

home as a centre of activities

home as a refuge from the outside world

home as an indicator of personal status

home as material structure

home as a place to own. (Franklin, 1996, p. 89)

She continues:

To ignore the perspective of the dwelling as 'home' and its relationship to a sense of identity, well-being and autonomy is to deny its centrality in human life. (p. 90)

The consequent task is to use the buildings and facilities of a residential home in the way that creates the aspects of 'home' that are thought most important. Burton (1989) describes the transformation of a large, old institution. Thought was given to separating private from public space: an area was designed to be open and welcoming to the public with reception facilities and other rooms which could be booked by local organizations; the bedrooms, sitting rooms, dining rooms and bathrooms were private, for use by residents and staff, with others going in by invitation. In some residential homes, more typically those abroad, facilities for other older people who live in the area have been established on the same campus: these may take the form of a health clinic, gym, swimming pool or restaurant. Of course, there are further possibilities of having facilities used by other age groups, perhaps with an under-fives group having some sessions. Debate is needed as to whether there can be sufficient privacy for the residents and whether the use by people with common characteristics (in this case older people) leads to a vibrant community or a ghetto.

The residential home is the place where the residents live. There should not be complete freedom for anybody to call in whenever they want. To allow uncontrolled visiting is to remove the recognition that in the residents' home, the residents should have a say in who visits and how they want to receive them. Residents must be allowed to maintain their role as host and hostess.

It is also useful to take account of how people use space. It is common for residents to sit near the front door or the office, a part of wanting to know what is going on. This could lead to careful thinking about the function of reception areas: welcoming visitors and reception; security with oversight of visitors to check their authenticity; a place for residents to sit; notices for visitors or residents. Entrances to different types of homes will vary, in some residents could have their own front doors, in others, the residents' private areas may lead off a common reception hall. For example, there could be a residents' sitting area (whether lounge, reading or coffee room) adjoining the reception area, separated by glass panels; or the reception area could be a desk in what is like a small hotel foyer with chairs and tables around for people to sit and be party to what is going on.

Willcocks *et al.* (1987) have noted the way in which a move to a residential home threatens a person's identity by removing their social and territorial props. Further, they have shown the importance people attach in their living space to being able to control their immediate environment: heating, fresh air, light and electrical equipment.

Cairns and Cairns (1989, p. 177) describe choosing the right place to site a children's home. They wanted children to have access to 'basic urban facilities within walking distance', to 'be able to make their own way to local schools' but also 'be able to visit and be visited by friends'. They preferred a small town to a large one. They recognized some of the characteristics of the children:

> Large groups of children are, however, noisy (particularly those with disrupted early experience) and active. This dictated a large garden, a house far enough away from other householders to have its own 'insulation', and easy access to open country. (p. 177)

Some of this planning is at odds with today's priorities of 'small and local'. 'Keep homes small' has been the reaction to the regimentation found in many large residential establishments; 'keep homes local' is the consequence of recognizing that residents can lose contact with relatives and friends. I am not arguing for all residential homes to be placed once again away from communities but I do contend that 'fitness for purpose' in planning terms should not be constructed around a principle such as 'small and local' without pursuing other factors like space or insulation from immediate neighbours. Young people need enough room to find private spaces and places for activities inside and outside. The boundary with local communities can become problematic as other young people (or at times adults) from the community invade the home or the young people from the home are viewed as a nuisance in the locality. Planning of buildings and facilities must recognize the relationship between competing factors.

Buildings should be designed to be inclusive. Some people find many residential homes unacceptable because they do not have prayer rooms or separate kitchens for different types of food. In the main, new building of residential homes for older people has ensured wheelchair access and adequate facilities for people with physical disabilities. This is not typical with buildings for younger adults and children's homes.

Planning relates not only to the design of buildings but to their use. Residents may be excluded from the kitchen on hygiene grounds, perhaps demanded by environmental health inspectors; they may be prevented from chatting to cooks or cooking themselves. How is a balance to be negotiated between essential hygiene requirements and a satisfactory lifestyle?

At the core of this task of 'management of the environment' is that of trying to ensure that the physical resources of buildings, plant and facilities support the primary task of the establishment rather than militate against it. In what ways can buildings and plant be designed and used so that people are able to develop their skills, meet other people and manage their daily lives?

The task then is to try to create in a residential home whatever are regarded as the key characteristics cited from Franklin. The residential home is not, and should not aim to be, the same as a private home. Each residential home will differ in aim and design. The key is an understanding within each home of physical and psychological security.

Proximity to others, for example expectations that people sit alongside others in a lounge, does not lead to friendships. Indeed, persuading people to sit alongside others because it is good for them or 'will take them out of themselves' is likely to be counter-productive.

The layout of the buildings may not make it easy for people get to know others. That may seem strange in environments where often so much living takes place alongside others in lounges. The problem is that the lifestyle in residential homes differs markedly from the ways in which people get to know others in their own homes. The usual ways in which we get to know others are far more tentative than finding ourselves sitting alongside them for long spells of the day. Typically, people find ways to begin a process of getting to know others by brief contacts, perhaps outside the house, followed by invitations for a cup of tea. There is a move between private space and public which allows a testing to see whether this person is one you want to get to know better. Within a residential home there is limited private space and large amounts of sitting in day rooms with people because they are there, not because you want to sit with them. Friendships will flourish more easily in those places where residents have opportunities to meet a wide variety of people and select whom they want to see again. The sorts of facilities which encourage this are those such as:- reading rooms where residents go in and out to read the paper; restaurants or coffee shops; clubs or activities. (Clough 1998a, pp. 20–1)

The traditional split in old-age homes between private rooms and lounges in which residents have their own place makes any such manoeuvrability difficult. One resident described this:

I don't go and visit in other lounges. I don't know whether they appreciate me coming or nor. So I stopped visiting, though I have visited about three times. (Clough, 1981, p. 97)

In the same study a health visitor described the difficulty of trying to talk to one resident in a lounge and being 'embarrassed about whether or not to chat to other residents'.

Good enough lifestyles

In what we might imagine to be an ideal world, we envisage a system in which regulation is unnecessary: people will work hard and productively; the objectives of the organization will be met; and the people who receive the services, in our case the residents, will be delighted with what they get. In this imaginary world people will work well because they enjoy the work and know that it is important to residents.

Probably the imaginary world is dismissed as pie in the sky, and we return to the everyday mechanics of how to produce services with which people are satisfied. But this 'if only' perspective touches on fundamentals: can people be trusted? will they work well if left on their own? what conditions encourage good work? do we really need all this monitoring, quality assurance and regulation?

When the service provided for someone is not good enough, there is a tendency to blame an individual staff member. Throughout this book I have stressed that the service provided in the home is heavily influenced by context. For example, the task is not just defined by residents or staff; people outside the home influence the definition of what is to happen. In the best practice, the task is not imposed but develops from debate and negotiation between interested parties.

Moreover if the activity of providing services for other people is held in low esteem, the impact on those who live and work in the home, and so on the quality of service, is dramatic. Of course, the level of resources in terms of buildings, staff and facilities is a further major influence on quality.

Individual staff may be able to work well for short periods in inauspicious environments. In the end, the contextual factors exert their influence: good, consistent, reliable and continuing provision will not last in a negative or threatening environment.

Having recognized the importance of context, I return to another thread in this book, the difficulty inherent in defining 'good enough' care. Attempts to capture what this means may focus on principles such as 'treating people with dignity' or indicators of the principle, perhaps addressing people in ways that maintain their dignity. But a list of components may fail to convey the whole. The way in which I am addressed does matter to me, for example whether particular people call me 'Mr Clough' or 'Roger'. However, what matters as much, perhaps far more, is whether they talk to me in a tone or style that is friendly, interested and respectful. Can the indicators capture the subtleties of 'dignity' and, indeed, the differences in people's perceptions both of the importance to be attached to a particular principle and what the components of that principle are?

The pursuit of quality

The focus on quality is seductive. First, 'quality' is the sort of hurrah word that it is difficult to oppose, because we all want good quality services. Yet what comprises quality is disputed. Second, the means of producing quality, usually taken from industrial production, are presented as straightforward and mechanical.

Quality enthusiasts often have catchphrases like 'Quality in, quality out'. Presenting quality in a simplistic way allows the structures and the environment of the home to be ignored. It is as important to understand the context of quality and regulation as it is of residential care.

James (1992), writing of quality as 'an idea ripe for its time' (p. 38), sees it as part of central government's determination to achieve 'economy, efficiency and effectiveness' and 'value for money'. She considered at that time 'the heritage of the quality movement in Social Services Departments' to have four characteristics:

> It is top-down, driven essentially by financial, ideological and political imperatives.
>
> User views have had... little impact...
>
> Certain tools have been emphasized, such as performance indicators.
>
> The approach has been reactive rather than proactive, with the emphasis on inspection and sanctions rather than incentives and control. (p. 40)

'Quality', in her view, became used as 'a set of tools' to be used at a time of intense change and became an 'integrating concept' (p. 46). She notes also that both quality and inspection were part of a governmental strategy to move towards a free market in public services.

There is not space here to pursue the social and political background to the provision of welfare services. What matters today, and in particular for this discussion of residential care, is to understand the ideas and consider whether they are useful for practice. The starting point is to recognize that ideas and techniques, such as quality assurance and quality control, were developed as part of other processes. In that sense they never were neutral.

There has been a change of emphasis from that described by James in that over recent years approaches to quality have emphasized both user response and being proactive. Indeed, documents such as the Residential Forum's 1996 *Creating a Home from Home* almost appear to state that the ultimate test of quality is the way in which a service is perceived by residents, a statement to which I have suggested earlier that provisos should be added (p. 147). A review system known as inside quality assurance (IQA), has at its heart that ways have to be found to encourage residents and staff to express their views on life in the home. Youll (1993), in an early review of IQA, comments that it makes 'a very positive contribution to helping people – front-line staff, residents, relatives – to speak out'. Further, the involvement of different interest groups of residents, staff and outsiders 'appeals to people's sense of fairness' (p. 111). She recognizes that residents were cautious about speaking out but still concludes that there were significant developments in encouraging residents to participate.

Second, most attempts to introduce what are termed quality systems into residential homes try to ensure that quality is built into what happens rather than tested for later. The approach is one of emphasizing the input rather than checking on the outcome. The general literature on quality is full of statements that systems should be designed to get the product right first time.

Quality at work

The most insidious danger in quality approaches is that they *may* divert attention from the primary task of the organization. The home exists to provide good services for residents, not to prove itself in tests of quality.

If the work of the residential home is to be reviewed, it should be examined against the primary task. This is yet another reason for the insistence on the definition of the primary task. Too many reviews of residential care examine systems or practice without reference to what the place is trying to do. This may be the fault of the management of the home as well as the fault of inspectors or quality assessors. Such an approach is fundamentally destructive of good residential care because it fails to link the indicator of practice with the experience of practice.

When this happens, quality assurance becomes a set of procedures rather than a serious drive to high standards. Many people who work in residential homes are cynical of quality systems in that they seem to demand conformity to particular ways of recording activities. The nub of the criticism is that quality assurance may relate to whether people can demonstrate that procedures have been followed satisfactorily; the focus is said to be on the presentation of action, rather than on the action itself.

The criticism is an important one and relates to earlier criticisms of management styles. The energy of the organization, that is the energy of the staff who work in the residential home, can go into *presenting* performance in order to win contracts, convince inspectors, please relatives or satisfy external managers. Of course the management of a home cannot ignore the need to package the goods, that is to present the product to others. However, the core of the activity and therefore the focus of energy must go into the activity for which the home exists. Quality systems should support that focus, not distract from it.

Crosby was one of the American gurus of the quality movement. Caulkin (1998) shows that Crosby is dismissive of the reliance on systems to achieve quality.

What happened to quality? The quality profession?' snorts Philip Crosby. 'They forget that quality isn't procedures: it's a philosophy.

Crosby contends that 'a profound idea' has been reduced to a set of 'box-ticking exercises'.

These... encourage the notion that quality is about techniques and systems. 'But techniques and systems don't accomplish anything by themselves... Management has to do that.'

To underline the difference he compares managing quality to driving a car. In a car... there is an instrument panel and... an instruction manual. They represent quality control and quality assurance respectively.

But neither of these makes the driver good or bad – it's how you use the car that does that. 'What happened to quality is that companies got awards for the instrument panel and the instruction manual... But what causes accidents – driver judgement and philosophy or the instruments?' (Caulkin, 1998, p. i)

Understanding this debate is critical to examining whether 'quality management' has anything to offer residential care. To be of value in residential care, quality management has to be understood in terms of a philosophy that drives the organization. The systems and procedures are then designed to implement or support that philosophy; if the systems become separated from the philosophy, the consequence is that the records they produce are useless.

All companies face the same issues, and almost all of them are about people: making them aware of the philosophy of quality and equipping them to act on it on the one hand and insisting that the philosophy is adhered to on the other. (Caulkin, 1998, p. iv)

The fundamental to be taken from this discussion is that neither a particular system nor requirements from an external source should drive the work in the residential care home. Good residential care is produced not by a single management approach but by clarity and agreement about the primary task and core values. Within the home as an organization, people have to determine the ways in which the task will be carried out. 'Quality management' is one such way.

This brings me back to one of my key arguments. If quality assurance is to be of use in promoting good practice, then definition of terms and development of systems must follow from discussion, debate and negotiation. A top-down assertion of the components of quality is of no use. In this brief passage lies the secret of whether systems are to be of value in residential care. Systems are not good in themselves: quality assurance, quality control, registration and inspection are of value only if they support an end product of vibrant residential care.

Some may see such systems as necessary evils: staff have to jump through hoops placed by others; the way to survive is to go through the motions and do as little as possible. I prefer a different approach: to look for ways in which quality assurance and regulation can be used purposefully.

Quality in residential care

Kelly and Warr (1992, p. 3) state that 'At its simplest, quality is about meeting agreed individual needs.' They give examples: 'a minibus which arrives on time to transport users safely' to a centre; a clean, single bedroom in a home; or 'genuine choice on aspects of living'. In earlier chapters I have emphasized the fact that the quality of residential practice is shown in the detail of the arrangements for daily living, basically in the combination of what is done and the way in which it is done. This recognizes process as a significant aspect of the task. In effect, I am adding the dimension of 'how it is done' to the examples above: the manner in which staff do their work, evidenced in the way staff speak to residents or make time available for them.

'Quality', writes James, 'is simply a social construct with meaning attached to it.'

> So, for some quality is about users; for others it is about staff performance; for others about information systems and task, and so on... It is everybody's distant cousin and nobody's baby. (1992, p. 50)

In this lie two of the central dilemmas for any organization which has responsibility for a product which is in large measure an activity between staff member and individual: how should the task be described so that there is clarity between different people as to what is intended? and, second, how should the activity be examined to see whether it has been undertaken in the way which was wanted? Quality has to be defined and then it has to be measured.

Quality care

The Residential Forum (1996) sets out the basic ingredients likely to be included in any quality assurance system in residential care:

An explicit and clear purpose for the Home

Defined requirements for the service and the success criteria

Defined process for achieving the requirements

Clear procedures for staff

Training programmes for all staff in quality assurance

Monitoring and recording systems

Auditing procedures and feedback for corrective action review and evaluation systems. (p. 52)

The authors point out that 'Quality assurance systems have been successful in highlighting ways in which improvements can be made for inputs and outputs' (p. 52). However, they stress that it is important to include processes and outcomes as part of quality systems. 'Addressing outcomes and service processes involves consideration of aspects which are more difficult to predict, monitor and measure' (p. 52). Immediately we examine the list above we move into the uncertain territory of presentation and result. The items listed are those factors which are thought to be essential in good quality assurance systems. But, as Crosby pointed out in the quotation earlier, the key to high quality lies not in being able to tick that certain things are in place; rather the secret is to be found in whether procedures such as these help to deliver the primary task.

In a later publication on management, the Residential Forum (1997, pp. 91, 95) has a fuller review of various systems for quality assurance and stresses the importance of involving staff, service users, relatives and representatives. As well as a useful discussion of current systems, the document sets out some reasons for introducing quality assurance systems. Thus, the writers ask whether service users will benefit, the image of the home be improved or there are sound business reasons for the introduction of a system (p. 93). They have a basic question: 'Why should we do this?' It is this question which has to be answered to the satisfaction of all parties and there is a danger, even in this review by the Residential Forum, that the mechanics of the system take priority over the value and purpose of quality assurance.

Being regulated

Another way in which attempts are made to ensure that homes are run appropriately is regulation, with its two components of registration and inspection. All places which carry out the functions of housing and care as defined in the Registered Homes Act 1984 (with the accompanying regulations for nursing homes, mental nursing homes and residential care homes) must be registered with the relevant body. It is an offence to run an unregistered home. Thus, whereas quality assurance is a voluntary activity, regulation is mandatory. The purpose of regulation is to give the state a means of ensuring that minimum standards are in place. Inspection is the process by which registered homes are examined; there are requirements that there should be both announced and unannounced inspections.

Regulation, like quality assurance, has to be seen in the context of social systems and social policy. In a free market, consumers want to know that the products they get are safe and conform to the claims made by manufacturers. In part, social care regulators fulfil the functions of trading standards officers or environmental health inspectors. Such regulation is recognized to be essential when those purchasing a service are unlikely to be able to test its quality or when failure to work to appropriate standards imposes a risk to health. Food hygiene requirements exist to try to prevent outbreaks like the *E. coli* epidemic in Scotland.

Of course any regulation introduces debates as to whether it is needed and whether the regulators are testing the right things. The usual response to this is to assert the necessity for regulation but then to question the detail: 'I know you need to know how we work, but surely you do not have to call just when we are rushed off our feet as the residents are going to bed.' Those subject to regulation often demand a greater reliance on their internal systems; they want to be left more on their own provided that they can demonstrate that they have quality assurance systems.

The context of inspection can be examined more fully elsewhere (Clough, 1994, pp. 1–46). Here I want to note some of the tensions inherent in the activity, before looking at the impact on, first, those inside the home and then the inspectors.

Tensions in regulation

At a rational level most of us will recognize the need for regulation. However, when we are the subjects of such regulatory activity we are likely to find the activity a nuisance and a threat, while still recognizing that it is necessary. Outsiders are coming to look at what we do:

- Will they understand and agree with our aims?
- Will they focus on what we think of as inessentials?
- How will we compare to others?
- How will others respond to the inspectors?
- Will they be able to write up what they find in words which we accept?

These are legitimate concerns. At worst, inspections are clumsily managed, intrusive and unhelpful towards evaluating what really matters. The conclusions drawn from OFSTED reports seem to me too often like this, when spurious claims of certainty are made by senior inspectors as to teaching methods or the quality of their own information. By contrast, some individual inspections of schools are well managed and allow all participants to learn from an evaluation. I stress again that regulation is important and necessary: the way it is carried out may be good or bad, effective or ineffective. The existence of regulators does not ensure that residential homes are good places in which to live.

Burton (1998) recognizes the potential of inspection: 'when inspection is truly independent (and seen to be so), it can become both the support and means by which all other outsiders could participate in the protection of residents and the development of Homes' (p. 222). However, he follows this with a scenario in which inspectors fail to examine complaints from a member of staff and where powerful individuals effectively block all channels of complaint or processes of change. It is not my task to evaluate the effectiveness of inspection units but the discussion here must acknowledge the doubts expressed by some as to their integrity and competence. Lest this be seen as knocking inspection units, it should be noted that I write this as someone who worked in just such an inspection unit for three and a half years and believes that they can work well.

The details of the regulatory task are to be found in two general guides to good practice: *Creating a Home from Home* (Residential Forum, 1996, pp. 6–7, 54, 96–100); and *A Better Home Life* (Centre for

Policy on Ageing, 1996, pp. 3, 123–8). The nature of regulatory activity is examined in *Insights into Inspection*, which looks at inspection through the eyes of residents, managers and inspectors. Noting the tensions, it sets out how the task can be done well.

> Wholesome inspection demands that the ways in which inspectors collect the information for their report are ones which promote the very qualities which the inspectorate thinks matter in establishments: they are concerned with the nature of relationships, the way inspectors talk to and about others, their willingness to listen, their ability to be aware of their own feelings but not to be consumed or driven by them. (Clough, 1994, pp. 167–8)

Managing inspections from inside a residential home

The title of this section may seem contradictory: staff and residents cannot manage an inspection; inspectors, with statutory authority, do that. At one level this is true, but insiders can work out what they want from inspections and how to present their demands.

It would be naive or foolhardy to expect staff to welcome the arrival of inspectors. Inspection does interfere with day-to-day life and does arouse strong feelings. Some of the points made by staff about inspection in one study were:

> bewilderment and confusion because no one knew what was expected;
>
> fear and anxiety as people felt under scrutiny and subject to personal criticism;
>
> anger about the intrusiveness of the process or the preoccupation with detailed administrative procedures;
>
> relief that it had gone smoothly;
>
> disappointment that the important issues had been ignored;
>
> pleasure at finding another channel to try and get things improved. (Clough, 1994, p. 36)

And there were further feelings when the reports arrived. The underlying concerns were whether they were accurate and fair, and whether inspectors had discussed with insiders the points which they wrote in reports (p. 37).

The task for managers, having recognized that regulation is necessary and therefore fundamentally accepted, is to make the activity as productive as possible: 'How can we use this intrusion into our lives in ways which are useful to what we are doing here?' becomes the question. I am not suggesting that the seeming nuisance of the inspection can be totally dispensed with; I am arguing for finding ways in which insiders can make best use of the activity of regulation in pursuit of the core activity of the place. This approach gives insiders some control in what otherwise seems an area of their lives which is beyond their influence.

The first requirement is to establish a realistic assessment of the value and the place of regulation. This demands:

- *understanding the task of regulation*, that is what it exists to do; auditors work to ensure the financial integrity of the system; inspectors are necessary to ensure the caring integrity; myths have to be examined and dispelled; in the end inspectors should not be viewed as enemies.

- *understanding the authority of inspectorates:* residents and staff should be clear as to the rights and powers of both inspectors and themselves; they should know how to question the ways in which inspectors are working or how to complain about them.

Reading the documentation of the inspectorate is important preparation, as is reading further material which examines regulation.

All staff should have a general understanding of the functions of inspectorates and so should as many residents as possible. There will need to be discussion as to which outsiders should be involved.

Second, the insiders should review their own activities on a regular basis. In some homes such review will be part of a quality system. The review allows insiders to develop a realistic view of the quality of work in the home and may well be carried out as part of regular events, such as meetings of residents, staff or relatives. The realistic view of the work should allow the insiders to feel confident in their work. Their task at inspections is to help the inspectors see the place as it really is.

Following this review *insiders plan to present their activities to outsiders*. In effect, people are saying to inspectors; 'In judging us, take account of the fact that we are trying to do this... We think a good measure of what we achieve is found in... We are aware that we can improve what we do in... and so are planning the following... We are struggling to work out what to do about... and would welcome your comments.'

It is particularly important, although I recognize hard to do, not to create the impression among staff or residents that the task is to cover up failings, to hide grubby corners or activities. In the end the anxiety to put a gloss on activities and to keep certain aspects secret is counter-productive to being confident when inspected. The culture of being open and willing to learn, which I have been arguing for in this book, should be maintained. There is no place for notions of a mistaken loyalty which demands that bad practice is hidden. I am aware that this will sound too easy: inspections should not be used as an opportunity to have debates with colleagues that should take place elsewhere, nor are they an occasion for settling old scores. The loyalty wanted is loyalty to the integrity of the task.

I remember in my first job as a teacher/housemaster in an approved school being on duty one evening when inspectors from the Department of Education were present. The head had decided to have a special evening activity. I cannot remember the exact nature of the event but I know that the boys enjoyed it. One of the first questions from the inspector to the boys was, 'How often do you have events like this?' 'Never had one before', came the reply. It is tempting but mistaken to put on a performance.

So, fourth, the aim is *to create a viable working relationship with regulators*, having sufficient confidence in the work of the home and being willing to listen to the views of others on the work in the home. Having people in the home who are interested in the work can be stimulating: the act of trying to explain to outsiders may clarify what is important and the consequent discussion may introduce alternative approaches. I still recall the trepidation with which as a teacher I received the information that an education inspector was to come into the classroom. As a teacher in an approved school, I felt isolated from others. The interest of the inspector and the comments made about ways I could do things differently, turned an anxious experience into a helpful one.

The final point I want to make about being subject to inspection, is to consider reviewing the work of the inspectors. One group of staff at a school read the guidelines for an impending inspection, noting the objectives and methods to be used. At the end of the inspection, they compiled a report on the work of the inspectors, commenting on performance against stated objectives. The idea behind such an approach is that it is reasonable to comment back to inspectors on perceptions of how they have worked. Again, this gives the insiders a measure of control. In particular, it is useful to report something that was unsatisfactory about inspections, and to suggest alternative approaches. As with any feedback, reporting regularly on what is good, makes reporting on what is not good more acceptable.

Inspectors have to present evidence for their conclusions. Insiders should challenge aspects of inspectors' reports where they disagree with fact or interpretation. All parties may be in agreement on what is to be achieved, such as providing individualized care. Inspectors may fix on certain means to achieve an end and become oblivious to alternatives. They may see it as a failing that there is no key worker system in operation; the staff and residents may have worked out a different way to provide individualized care.

Implications for inspectors

Inspectors are likely to feel vulnerable and under pressure, although this may not appear so to those inside the establishment. The inspectors will be only too aware that drawing conclusions from what they find is risky: they know they may make incorrect judgements. For example, they may conclude that a place is working well, only to be proven wrong later; or vice versa. One temptation for inspectors is to be non-committal. In this scenario, factual information such as size of rooms and number of bathrooms is reported precisely, but conclusions about the quality of care or relationships between staff and residents are avoided. Making judgements is risky and it is more risky to report that something is 'good' or 'bad', rather than 'satisfactory'. Some try to avoid any judgement and limit themselves to stating what changes could be made.

Inspectors, like residential staff, need to remind themselves of the importance of their work: it is concerned with protection of people and the development of good practice. Given a fundamental belief in what they are doing, then inspectors have to pursue their task with integrity: examining what others do and, in the process, being willing to question, search and challenge. To do that, they must retain their independence.

This is not the place for a treatise on regulation. However, the relevance of this book for inspection is that inspectors need to understand the experience of living and working in a residential home. They must listen and learn. They must be mindful of working in ways which support the best practice they want to promote. To create a climate of openness, they must be open.

Evaluation

Evaluation, whether by insiders or outsiders, should not claim certainty. It should be the best judgement at that time. Inspectors should try to understand what a place is trying to achieve and the way in which it works. A.S. Neill, the founder of Summerhill, at that time a school in the forefront of progressive education, told inspectors: 'You can't really inspect Summerhill because our criteria are happiness, sincerity, balance and sociability.' The inspectors reported that Neill thought:

> his school must stand or fall rather by the kind of children that it allows its pupils to grow into, than by the specific skills and abilities that it teaches them. On the basis of evaluation it may be said:
>
> 1. That the children are full of life and zest.
>
> 2. That the children's manners are delightful.
>
> 3. That initiative, responsibility and integrity are all encouraged by the system.
>
> 4. That such evidence as is available does not suggest that the products of Summerhill are unable to fit into ordinary society when they leave the school. (Neill, 1962, p. 85)

However, they also reported on the quality of teaching:

> To have created a situation in which academic education of the most intelligent kind could flourish is an achievement, but in fact it is not flourishing and a great opportunity is thus being lost...
>
> There remains in the mind some doubts both about principles and about methods. A closer and longer acquaintance with the School would perhaps remove some of these and intensify others. (Neill, 1962, p. 86)

Neill counters with evidence of academic achievement in the numbers of exams passed but asserts that academic achievement was not the prime goal of the school.

The discussion is of particular interest because 50 years on from that report, Summerhill's future has once again been called into question, in part as a consequence of inspectors' reports.

Impressively, the inspectors were willing to judge the place on the school's own criteria. But they added external views of education. Both perspectives are important. A tension is apparent as well as to both the purpose of education (a happy, balanced sociable person, in Neill's terms as opposed to scholastic achievement) and the methods of education. The inspectors make these differences explicit and are willing to state their concerns, recognizing that further study would be needed to check out some of their anxieties. To use a teaching metaphor, there are lessons for inspectors of residential care and nursing homes.

Presentation

Certain outsiders have a legitimate interest in the quality of care in a home: prospective residents, relatives, those purchasing residential care on behalf of a public authority and, possibly, neighbours and other professionals. How are they to get their information? How are the insiders to present themselves?

The reference point has to be the primary task of the establishment. The purpose of presentation is not to get accolades, nor is it to deceive. The purpose should be to find ways in which outsiders with a legitimate right can get an accurate picture of the home, but at the same time to protect the integrity of the work. The place about which outsiders want information is the place where residents live: it is their home. The boundary of the home needs protection.

Differing objectives vie with each other for attention: openness and privacy; security and freedom. The task in each home in relation to outsiders is to work out how to be sufficiently open *and* sufficiently private. The following is an example of a general statement, to which specifics would be added:

> Within the home, the residents and staff try to provide a place where people can... (*a brief statement on purpose/task would be added in relation to a particular home*). We are happy for other people to know how we work, and think it essential that anyone who plans to live here should be able to find that out before moving in. In this sense, we want to be open, letting others see us as we are. The way we work changes as we learn from each other, and we would want to learn from visitors as, we hope, they may be able to learn from us.
>
> However, this place is the residents' home and we want to protect their privacy. Therefore we (again that is residents and staff) have worked out the following arrangements for visitors... (*The notes would then refer to different types of visitors, relatives and friends, work visitors (social workers, doctors), inspectors, prospective residents, independent visitors, perhaps others from the local community*).

Inspectors have a statutory right to visit at any time. That apart, we would ask others to follow our guidelines, let us know if they are inconvenient and negotiate any changes.

You may also like to know that the following information on the home is available in pamphlets or on the world wide web:

- a statement of the way we work;
- internal reviews and annual reports;
- the reports of the external inspectorate with responsibility for registration;
- arrangements for residents, including terms and contract.

Of course, the best way to get to know the home is to visit and to talk to residents and staff. Our usual time for such visits is…

Speaking out

It will be apparent from earlier comment that one of the dangers in residential work is that of secrecy. The discrepancy in power between resident and staff means that residents may be put under pressure to keep quiet about their concerns. By contrast, the manager has to establish with residents and staff that the overriding loyalty is to the welfare of residents, a task that requires freedom to comment on any aspect of life in the home.

Thus 'freedom to talk' is one way to challenge bullying. As part of a wider culture, it is a positive aspect of an environment in which people recognize that they can continue to learn about other people and ways of working in residential homes.

Attempts to counter bad practice

By contrast with attempts to identify the conditions for effective practice, much of current management practice in welfare services is a response to the failings of services. There has been a powerful critique of such services in general and of residential care in particular. The presumption appears to have been that the services have not produced the desired ends because of lax control by managers and poor work by staff. The answer of many people, in the managerialist style of the 1980s and 90s, has been found in clearer specification of the task, in an active style of management that examines the work undertaken, and in the calling of people to account for their work. Indeed, the split of functions between purchaser and provider is in part premised on the same grounds: if a contract sets out what people should be providing, then it becomes easier to examine whether the service is provided in the ways that were laid down. The argument for this approach rests on beliefs in the need to control staff.

One part of the argument for such control has been that workers have exerted too much power so that the work activity was distorted. Managers, the same argument would run, either were not able to direct staff or did not know how to do it. There is no doubt that there have been examples of the work activity dictated by staff to the detriment of the care of residents. The report into Nye Bevan Lodge, a home for older people, stated that staff were often watching afternoon TV and did not look after the residents; they charged the residents for some services; they threatened some residents and punished them if their behaviour did not conform (Gibbs *et al.*, 1987). Sadly, many other examples of bad practice exist, a factor which must be recognized in any analysis of work and management.

However, there is a legitimate debate as to whether a controlling management style produces the high quality care that is wanted. I argue that attempts to prevent bad practice by increased control are mistaken and ineffective. They are likely to ignore the complexities of residential care which have been discussed extensively throughout this book: who is to do what for whom? what sort of holding and touching is appropriate? Further, they are likely to ignore the impact of external structures: the prevailing culture of the wider organization; staff pay and conditions; the resources (buildings, staffing and money) and the confused expectations of society as to what is to happen in a residential home. Managerialism does not achieve the desired ends.

This is not to argue that we should not learn from bad practice. Rather, the question is: 'What is it that is to be learnt?' First, bad practice has to be defined in relation to the task and to good practice. It is no good trying to stop things happening without considering what ought to happen. Thus, the manager has to negotiate with stakeholders to set out expectations. What should be attempted is to link values with practice. It is not possible to prescribe what staff would do in every eventuality; indeed, attempts to define actions in minute segments inappropriately freeze responses. Therefore, staff and others have to know the core values and style expected within the home so that they are in a position to work out what to do in specific circumstances.

There are other pointers to what ought to happen from the conditions in which bad practice can thrive. First, it is imperative that all parties understand the nature of the enterprise: what is to be expected within the home in terms of values, style, skills and, consequently, daily living? There is evidence that sometimes people have tolerated abuse because they did not know that such practices should not have taken place.

It is also essential for all parties to try to distinguish 'not good enough care' from bad care which must be stopped immediately. For example, an adult may need help in going to the lavatory; she/he may call for assistance when they want to leave; an immediate response is ideal, a short wait is acceptable. Somewhere on a continuum, the period of waiting becomes unacceptable. 'The word *abuse* is vague until linked with other words in phrases such as "abuse of power"' (Clough, 1999, p. 206). Precision in defining terms is important.

Another factor in preventing abuse is that all stakeholders (but residents and staff in particular) know what to do if they are dissatisfied with practice; this relates to informal process as well as formal procedure. There must be complaints procedures which are well publicized and easy to use.

Understanding the causation of abuse is also useful. I have identified four major explanations, *structural*, and *environmental* factors interacting with the *individual characteristics* of staff and residents and the *work-style* of the staff group (Clough, 1999, p. 215). The structural explanation recognizes the ways in which economic and other forces structure perceptions so that concerns of older people are given less importance than those of children or younger adults. Environmental factors are the conditions in which people live and work, for example the state of the buildings, or staffing numbers and capacities. However, recognizing the potential significance of structures and environment must not lead to ignoring the impact of individuals, whether staff or residents. Some people are more likely to abuse than others. Finally, the work-style category acknowledges that staff are not just vessels at the mercy of the elements: they have a capacity to determine their approach to work.

Management has the responsibility to create the conditions in which the primary task of the home can be accomplished. In the same way management should aim to counter the factors noted above which contribute to abuse. Writing on homes for older people, I have suggested that management should aim to create:

- *in relation to structures,* a climate in which the belittling of old people is challenged and their views are taken seriously; further, the contracts with individual residents are detailed, clearly written and specify what residents should do if they want to discuss their care;

- *in relation to environment,* a setting in which people can live and work well: appropriate buildings, plant and facilities; clarity about the task; sufficient staff to undertake the job as defined by the expectations of residents, regulators and so of the management itself;

- *in relation to individual staff and residents,* systems for the appointing of staff which have the best chance of keeping out inappropriate people; systems to support staff; procedures for observing and thinking about individual residents, in particular those who may be most vulnerable;

- *in relation to worker-style,* a staff team which has its first loyalty to the care of residents and works openly, so challenging the secrecy on which abuse thrives. (Clough, 1999, pp. 215–16, adapted)

Managers need to be involved in day-to-day living, indeed in work with residents. The reasons for this activity are not only that managers have skills that they could be using. By 'doing', managers can pick up clues about life and practice in the home: they will see and hear how residents are; and they will learn about the current climate in the home.

Living, listening and learning

Dingleton Mental Illness Hospital at Melrose was transformed under Maxwell Jones into a therapeutic community. I had a short placement there as a student in 1965 and I remember Maxwell Jones, the director, wanting to introduce a motto for the establishment. Perhaps today we would term this 'a mission statement', although it would have to be said that mottoes have the great advantage over many mission statements of being somewhat shorter. In what later writers would have described as getting staff involved in defining the goals of the organization under change, he asked staff to discuss the matter. The outcome was the phrase *Living and learning.* At Dingleton it would have been recognized that people learn from each other, staff from patients and staff, patients from staff and patients. Such learning is not dependent on hierarchy.

Indeed, it is apparent that learning involves listening not only in the formal sense of asking for feedback from people but in an active way of searching to understand. This is one of the key attributes of successful residential homes. Perhaps it could be seen as a part of

Morgan's metaphor of the organization as 'brain'. A metaphor for an organization for residential work could be an *ear*, provided that this includes the activity of trying to understand and process.

Writing recently about football management, Collins (1998) compared the qualities that make managers successful:

> There are certain definable traits of the successful manager. We remember the passion of Bill Shankly, the disciplinarianism of Brian Clough, the almost priestly aura of Sir Matt Busby, the work ethic of Ferguson. What they all share with Wenger is that, despite their public personas, behind the dressing room door they are prepared to listen and learn within the parameters of their immutable tenets.

One footballer quoted in the article, Ian Wright, said: 'He treats people like adults and gets the best out of them.'

In conclusion

The managers of residential homes must believe in and uphold the importance of the task of providing housing and services for people who want them. They must also believe that the task can be fulfilled in ways which are morally good, that is with practices in which they have confidence. Some of the problems faced by residents may be beyond the capacity of the home to put right: residents may not have supportive families in which they are cherished; their capacity to manage the activities of daily living may not be recoverable; sadness over tragic life events cannot be taken away. Yet nobody should be involved in managing or working in a residential care home if they do not believe that the work can be done well.

The fundamental for management – and for residential care – is to support the overriding purpose for which the place exists, that is the primary task. Different words such as therapeutic, healing or caring may be used to describe the style or purpose. The imperative is that residential homes are good places in which residents may live.

Bibliography

Atkinson D. (1989) Group homes for people with mental handicap: key issues for everyday living, in Brown A. and Clough R. (eds) *Groups and Groupings: Life and Work in Day and Residential Centres*, London: Routledge.

Atherton J. (1989) *Interpreting Residential Life: Values to Practise*, London: Tavistock/Routledge.

Balbernie R. (1975) Foreword, in Millham S., Bullock R. and Cherrett P. *After Grace – Teeth*, London: Chaucer.

Barr H. (1987) *Perspectives on Training for Residential Work*, London: CCETSW.

Barton R. (1959) *Institutional Neurosis*, Bristol: John Wright.

Beedell C. (1970) *Residential Life with Children*, London: Routledge & Kegan Paul.

Beedell C. (1996) Learning from experience about therapeutic work, *Therapeutic Communities*, **17**: 4.

Beedell C. and Clough R. (1992) Evidence for the inquiry into the selection and recruitment of staff in children's homes (Warner Committee), unpublished.

Berridge D. (1997) *Foster Care: A Research Review*, London: HMSO.

Blakemore K. (1989) Does age matter? The case of old age in minority ethnic groups, in Bytheway B. *et al.* (eds) *Becoming and Being Old*, London: Sage.

Blakemore K. (1993) Ageing and ethnicity, in Johnson J. and Slater R. (eds) *Ageing and Late Life*, London: Sage.

Blakemore K. and Boneham M. (1993) *Age, Race and Ethnicity in Britain*, Milton Keynes: Open University Press.

Bland R. (ed.) (1996) *Developing Services for Older People and their Families*, London: Jessica Kingsley.

Bond J., Briggs R. and Coleman P. (1993) The study of ageing, in Bond J., Coleman P. and Peace S. (eds) *Ageing in Society*, London: Sage.

Bowlby J. (1969) *Attachment and Loss: Attachment*, vol. 1, London: Tavistock.

Braithwaite J. (1993) Beyond positivism: learning from contextual integrated strategies, *Journal of Research in Crime and Delinquency*, **30**(4): 383–99.

Brown A. and Clough R. (eds) (1989) *Groups and Groupings: Life and Work in Day and Residential Centres*, London: Routledge.

Brown E., Bullock R., Hobson C. and Little M. (1998) *Making Residential Care Work: Structure and Culture in Children's Homes*, Aldershot: Ashgate.

Bullock R., Little M. and Millham S. (1993) *Residential Care for Children: A Review of the Research*, London: HMSO.

Burn M. (1967) *Mr Lyward's Answer: A Successful Experimentation in Education*, London: Hamish Hamilton.

Burton J. (1989) Institutional change and group action, in Brown A. and Clough R. (eds) *Groups and Groupings: Life and Work in Day and Residential Centres*, London: Routledge.

Burton J. (1998) *Managing Residential* Care, London: Routledge.

Butrym Z. (1976) The Nature of Social Work, London: Macmillan.

Cain P. (1998) Learning through philosophy, in Ward A. and McMahon L. (eds) *Intuition is not Enough*, London: Routledge.

Cairns B. and Cairns K. (1989) The family as a living group, in Brown A. and Clough R. (eds) *Groups and Groupings: Life and Work in Day and Residential Centres*, London: Routledge.

Caplan G. (1964) *Principles of Preventative Psychiatry*, New York: Basic Books.

Carter P., Jeffs T. and Smith M. (eds) (1989) *Social Work and Social Welfare Yearbook 1*, Milton Keynes: Open University Press.

Caulkin S. (1998) It's not ticking boxes or following procedures – quality is a philosophy, *The Observer*, 7 June.

CCETSW (Central Council for Education and Training in Social Work) (1973) *Residential Work is Part of Social Work*, London: CCETSW.

CCETSW (1995) *Assuring Quality in the Diploma in Social Work – 1, Rules and Requirements for the DipSW*, London: CCETSW.

Centre for Policy on Ageing (1996) *A Better Home Life*, London: Centre for Policy on Ageing.

Clark, H., Dyer S. and Horwood J. (1998) *'That Bit of Help': The High Value of Low Level Preventative Services for Older People*, London: The Policy Press in association with Community Care.

Clough R. (1970) The History of Reformatory and Approved Schools, MPhil. thesis, London: University of London.

Clough R. (1981) *Old Age Homes*, London: Allen & Unwin.

Clough R. (1982) *Residential Work*, Basingstoke: Macmillan.

Clough R. (1988) *Living Away from Home*, Bristol: University of Bristol.

Clough R. (1990) *Practice, Politics and Power in Social Services Departments*, Aldershot: Gower.

Clough R. (1993) Housing and services for older people, in Day P. (ed.) *Perspectives on Later Life*, London: Whiting & Birch.

Clough R. (ed.) (1994) *Insights into Inspection: The Regulation of Social Care*, London: Whiting & Birch.

188   *Bibliography*

Clough R. (1996a) Homes for heroines and heroes? hotels for pensioners? housing and care for older people, Inaugural lecture, Lancaster: Lancaster University.

Clough R. (1996b) The transmission of culture within residential care, in FICE *Fostering Cultural Diversity in a Turbulent World: A Challenge to Extra Familial Care*, Copenhagen: Ministry of Social Affairs.

Clough R. (1996c) Children in desperate need: their placement in specialist residential settings. Unpublished research report. Lancaster: Lancaster University.

Clough R. (1997) The training needs of direct care workers with children and young people, in *A Report on a Workshop on Options for the Future*, London: NISW.

Clough R. (1998a) *Living in Someone Else's Home*, London: Counsel and Care.

Clough R. (1998b) Scandalous care: interpreting public enquiry reports of scandals in residential care, *Journal of Elder Abuse and Neglect*, **10**(1–2): 13–27.

Clough R. (1999) The abuse of older people in institutional settings: the role of management and regulation in Stanley N., Manthorpe J. and Penhale B., *Institutional Abuse: Perspectives Across the Life Course*, London: Routledge.

Clough R. and Parsloe P. (eds) (1989) *Squaring the Circle*, Bristol: University of Bristol.

Coleman P. (1993) Adjustment in later life, in Bond J., Coleman P. and Peace S. (eds) *Ageing in Society*, London: Sage.

Counsel and Care (1995) *Last Rights*, London: Counsel and Care.

Cumbria Social Services Inspectorate (undated) *Residential Care Homes Handbook*, Carlisle: Cumbria County Council.

Cumming E. and Henry W. (1961) *Growing Old: The Process of Disengagement*, New York: Basic Books.

Davies B. and Knapp M. (1981) *Old People's Homes and the Production of Welfare*, London: Routledge & Kegan Paul.

Day P. (ed.) (1993) *Perspectives on Later Life*, London: Whiting & Birch.

Despres C. (1991) The meaning of home: literature review and directions for future research and theoretical development, *Journal of Architectural and Planning Research*, **8**(2): 96–115.

Dockar-Drysdale B. (1973) *Consultations in Child Care: Collected Topics*, London: Longman.

DoH (Department of Health) (1989) *Homes are for Living In*, London: HMSO.

Erikson E. (1950) *Childhood and Society*, New York: Norton.

Fenton S. (1986) *Race, Health and Welfare; Afro-Caribbeans and South Asian People in Central Bristol*, Bristol: University of Bristol.

Ford J. and Sinclair R. (1987) *Sixty Years On: Women Talk About Old Age*, London: The Women's Press.

Franklin B. (1996) New perspectives on housing and support for older people, in Bland R. (ed.) *Developing Services for Older People and their Families*, London: Jessica Kingsley.

Gibbons J. (1988) Mentally ill, in Sinclair I. (ed.) *Residential Care: The Research Reviewed*, London: HMSO.

Gibbs J., Evans M. and Rodway S. (1987) *Report of the Inquiry into Nye Bevan Lodge*, London: London Borough of Southwark Social Services Department.

Gilbert N. (ed.) (1992) *Researching Social Life*, London: Sage.

Goldberg E. and Hatch S. (eds) (1981) *A New Look at the Personal Social Services*, London: Policy Studies Institute.

Griffiths R. (1988) *Community Care: Agenda for Action*, London: HMSO.

Hadley R. and Clough R. (1996) *Care in Chaos: Frustration and Challenge in Community Care*, London: Cassell.

Hancock C. (1998) Interview, on *Today,* Radio 4, 5 August.

Hardiker P. (1989) quoted in Everitt *et al.* (1992) *Applied Research for Better Practice*, London: BASW/Macmillan.

Hare R. (1978) Moral philosophy, in Magee B. (ed.) *Men of Ideas*, London: British Broadcasting Operation.

Harlesden Community Project (1979) *Community Work and Caring for Children*, Ilkley: Owen Wells.

Hasenfeld Y (ed.) (1992) *Human Services as Complex Organisations*, California: Sage.

Havighurst R. (1963) Successful ageing, in Williams R., Tibbitts C. and Donahue W. (eds) *Processes of Ageing*, vol. 1, New York: Atherton Press.

Hill S. (1989) *A Change for the Better*, London: Hamish Hamilton.

Hudson J. (1985) The ethics of residential social work, in Watson D. (ed.) *A Code of Ethics for Social Work*, London: Routledge & Kegan Paul.

James A. (1992) Quality and its social construction by managers, in Kelly D. and Warr B. (eds) *Quality Counts*, London: Whiting & Birch/Social Care Association.

Johnson M. (1993) Dependency and independency, in Bond J., Coleman P. and Peace S. (eds) *Ageing in Society*, London: Sage.

Jones K. and Fowles A. (1984) *Ideas on Institutions*, London: Routledge & Kegan Paul.

Kahan B. (1994) *Growing Up in Groups*, London: HMSO.

Kelly D. and Warr B. (eds) (1992) *Quality Counts*, London: Whiting & Birch/Social Care Association.

Kennard D. (1983) *An Introduction to Therapeutic Communities*, London: Routledge & Kegan Paul.

King R., Raynes N. and Tizard J. (1971) *Patterns of Residential Care*, London: Routledge & Kegan Paul.

Knapp M. and Fenyo A. (1989) Economic perspectives on foster care, in Carter P., Jeffs T. and Smith M. (eds) *Social Work and Social Welfare Yearbook 1*, Milton Keynes: Open University Press.

Kubler-Ross E. (1969) *On Death and Dying*, New York: Macmillan.

Leat D. (1988) Younger physically disabled adults, in Sinclair I. (ed.) *Residential Care: The Research Reviewed*, London: HMSO.

Levy A. and Kahan B. (1991) *The Pindown Experience and the Protection of Children*, Stafford: Staffordshire County Council.

McEwan I. (1987) *The Child in Time*, London: Pan.

Magee B. (ed.) (1978) *Men of Ideas*, London: British Broadcasting Operation.

Maier H. W. (1981) Essential components in care and treatment environments for children, in Ainsworth F. and Fulcher L. (eds) *Group Care for Children*, London: Tavistock.

Marshall M. (1983) *Social Work with Old People*, London: Macmillan.

Menzies I. (1959) The functioning of social systems as a defence against anxiety: a report on a study of the nursing service of a general hospital, *Human Relations*, **13**: 95–121.

Menzies-Lyth I. (1988) *Containing Anxiety in Institutions. Selected Essays, Vol. 1*, London: Free Association Books.

Miller E. and Gwynne C. (1972) *A Life Apart*, London: Tavistock.

Millham S., Bullock R. and Cherrett P. (1975a) *After Grace – Teeth*, London: Chaucer.

Millham S., Bullock R. and Cherrett P. (1975b) Comparative analysis of residential institutions, in Tizard, J., Sinclair I. and Clarke R., *Varieties of Residential Experience*, London: Routledge & Kegan Paul.

Millham S., Bullock R. and Cherrett P. (1975c) Socialisation in residential communities, in Tizard, J., Sinclair I. and Clarke R., *Varieties of Residential Experience*, London: Routledge & Kegan Paul.

Millham S., Bullock R., Hosie K. and Haak M. (1986) *Lost in Care*, Aldershot: Gower.

Monsky S. (1963) *Staffing of Local Authority Residential Homes for Children*, London: Central Office of Information.

Morgan G. (1986) *Images of Organization*, California: Sage.

Morris J. (1993) *Community Care or Independent Living?* York: Joseph Rowntree.

Morris P. (1969) *Put Away*, London: Routledge & Kegan Paul.

Morris T. and Morris P. (1963) *Pentonville*, London: Routledge & Kegan Paul.

Morse J. (1994) *Critical Issues in Qualitative Research Methods*, Thousand Oaks, California: Sage.

Neill A. (1962) *Summerhill*, London: Penguin.

Parker R. (1981) Tending and social policy, in Goldberg E. and Hatch S. (eds) *A New Look at the Personal Social Services*, London: Policy Studies Institute.

Parker R. (1988) Children, in Sinclair I. (ed.) *Residential Care: The Research Reviewed*, London: HMSO.

Parkes C. (1986) *Bereavement: Studies of Grief in Adult Life* (2nd edn), London: Tavistock.

Parsloe P. (1989) Can you care for profit? in Clough R. and Parsloe P. (eds) *Squaring the Circle*, Bristol: University of Bristol.

Patti R. (1992) Preface, in Hasenfeld Y. (ed.) *Human Services as Complex Organisations*, California: Sage.

Payne M. (1985) The code of ethics, the social work manager and the organisation, in Watson D. (ed.) *A Code of Ethics for Social Work*, London: Routledge & Kegan Paul.

Payne M. (1995) *Social Work and Community Care*, Basingstoke: Macmillan.

Payne M. (1997) *Modern Social Work Theory* (2nd edn), Basingstoke: Macmillan.

Peace S. (ed.) (1998) *Involving Older People in Research*, London: Centre for Policy on Ageing.

Penna S., Paylor I. and Soothill K. (1995) *Job Satisfaction and Dissatisfaction: a Study of Residential Care Work*, London: National Institute for Social Work.

Peters T. and Waterman R. (1982) *In Search of Excellence*, New York: Harper & Row.

Pick P. (1981) *Children at Tree Tops*, London: Residential Care Association.

Pollitt C. (1993) *Managerialism and the Public Services. Cuts or Cultural Change in the 1990s?* Oxford: Blackwell.

Pottage D. and Evans M. (1994) *The Competent Workplace: The View from Within*, London: National Institute for Social Work.

Rapoport R. (1960) *Community as Doctor*, London: Tavistock.

Residential Forum (1996) *Creating a Home from Home; a Guide to Standards*, London: Residential Forum.

Residential Forum (1997) *Managing a Home from Home; a Companion to Creating a Home from Home*, London: Residential Forum.

Residential Forum (1998a) *Training for Social Care: Achieving Standards for the Undervalued Service*, London: Residential Forum.

Residential Forum (1998b) *A Golden Opportunity*, London: Residential Forum.

Robertson J. (1958) *Young Children in Hospital*, London: Tavistock.

Rowntree (1999) Low intensity support: preventing dependency, *Foundations*, York: Joseph Rowntree Foundation.

Sainsbury E., Nixon S. and Phillips D. (1982) *Social Work in Focus*, London: Routledge & Kegan Paul.

Sherman E. (1981) *Counselling the Aging: an Integrative Approach*, New York: Free Press.

Sinclair I. (ed.) (1988a) *Residential Care: The Research Reviewed*, London: HMSO.

Sinclair I. (1988b) Common issues in the client reviews, in Sinclair I. (ed.) *Residential Care: The Research Reviewed*, London: HMSO.

Sinclair I. (1988c) Elderly, in Sinclair I. (ed.) *Residential Care: The Research Reviewed*, London: HMSO.

Sinclair I., Crosbie D., O'Connor P., Stanforth L. and Vickery A. (1988) *Bridging Two Worlds: Social Work and the Elderly Living Alone*, Aldershot: Avebury.

Smith D. (1998) What counts as evidence and how should we use it? Conference paper at University of Dundee, 1 September.

Stein M. and Carey K. (1986) *Leaving Care*, Oxford: Blackwell.

Stevenson O. (1968) Reception into care – its meaning for all concerned, reprinted in Tod R. (ed.) *Children in Care*, London: Longmans.

Stevenson O. (1996) Changing practice: professional attitudes, consumerism and empowerment, in Bland R. (ed.) *Developing Services for Older People and their Families*, London: Jessica Kingsley.

Timms N. and Timms R. (1977) *Perspectives in Social Work*, London: Routledge & Kegan Paul.

Tizard J. (1975) Quality of residential care for retarded children in Tizard, J., Sinclair I. and Clarke R., *Varieties of Residential Experience*, London: Routledge & Kegan Paul.

Tizard, J., Sinclair I. and Clarke R. (1975) Introduction in Tizard, J., Sinclair I. and Clarke R., *Varieties of Residential Experience*, London: Routledge & Kegan Paul.

Tobin S. and Lieberman M. (1976) *Last Home for the Aged*, San Fransisco: Jossey Bass.

Tod R. (ed.) (1968) *Children in Care*, London: Longmans.

Townsend P. (1962) *The Last Refuge*, London: Routledge & Kegan Paul.

Tozer R. and Thornton P. (1995) *A Meeting of Minds: Older People as Research Advisers*, York: Social Policy Research Unit.

Triseliotis J. and Russell J. (1984) *Hard to Place: The Outcome of Residential Care and Adoption*, London: Heinemann.

Wagner Development Group (1993) *Positive Answers*, London: HMSO.

Wagner G. (chair) (1988) *A Positive Choice*, London: HMSO.

Ward A. (1996) Training: personal learning for professional practice, editorial in *Therapeutic Communities*, Winter 1996, **17**:4.

Ward A. (1998) The inner world and its implications, in Ward A. and McMahon L. (eds) *Intuition is not Enough*, London: Routledge.

Ward A. and McMahon L. (eds) (1998) *Intuition is not Enough*, London: Routledge.

Warner N. (chair) (1992) *Choosing with Care*, London: HMSO.

Watson D. (ed.) (1985) *A Code of Ethics for Social Work*, London: Routledge & Kegan Paul.

Whitaker D., Archer L. and Hicks L. (1998) *Working in Children's Homes: Challenges and Complexities*, Chichester: Wiley.

Whitaker D., Cook J., Dunne C. and Lunn-Rockliffe S. (1984) The experience of residential care from the perspectives of children, parents and care-givers, unpublished report to the ESRC, York: University of York.

Wilkin D. (1990) Dependency, in Peace S. (ed.) *Researching Social Gerontology*, London: Sage.

Willcocks D., Peace S. and Kellaher L. (1987) *Private Lives in Public Places*, London: Tavistock.

Williams Committee (1967) *Caring for People: Staffing Residential Homes*, London: Allen & Unwin.

Wolins M. (1974) *Successful Group Care*, Chicago: Aldine.

Youll P. (1993) The Caring in Homes Initiative, in Wagner Development Group *Positive Answers*, London: HMSO.

Index